Kate Delaney's book, *Deal Your Own Destiny*, will give you inspiration and a pathway to becoming MAD. By MAD, I mean making a difference in your life, in someone else's life, and in the world.

PHILIP J. ROMANO
Entrepreneur & Philanthropist, MAD
Founder, Fuddruckers & Romano's Macaroni Grill

Are you asking, "What's next?" Gain powerful examples of perseverance and grit from Kate Delaney's journey through 500 rejections and 780 locker rooms and into the office of the CEO. Reading Kate's book is like sitting down with a longtime trusted friend who has wisdom to share. This candid conversation will teach you how to stack your deck and will put you on the road to success.

RUBY NEWELL-LEGNER
Fan Engagement Expert
Founder, 7 Star Service

Kate Delaney's book is a game changer for anyone who wants to take control of their life and deal their own destiny. No matter where you are in your journey, this book will give you inspiration and the tools to help you get there. It's no surprise that she's a successful broadcaster and sought-after speaker.

ELLEN RATNER
White House Correspondent
Bureau Chief, Talk Media News

It's my pleasure to be on the air every day with Kate Delaney for ForbesBooks Radio, and trust me when I say that if anyone can teach you how to consistently look at the field, assess the odds, and execute the perfect winning play, it's her. Kate's trip to the top has been a wild ride, and in this book, she shares all of her stories and all of her lessons learned.

GREGG STEBBEN
ForbesBooks Radio

DEAL YOUR OWN DESTINY

— KATE DELANEY —

DEAL YOUR OWN DESTINY

Increase Your Odds, Win BIG and Become **Extraordinary**

ForbesBooks

Published by ForbesBooks, Charleston, South Carolina.
Member of Advantage Media Group.

ForbesBooks is a registered trademark, and the ForbesBooks colophon is a trademark of Forbes Media, LLC.

Printed in the United States of America.

10 9 8 7 6 5 4 3 2 1

ISBN: 978-19-46633-14-9
LCCN: 2018946022

Cover and layout design by Melanie Cloth.

This publication is designed to provide accurate and authoritative information in regard to the subject matter covered. It is sold with the understanding that the publisher is not engaged in rendering legal, accounting, or other professional services. If legal advice or other expert assistance is required, the services of a competent professional person should be sought.

Advantage Media Group is proud to be a part of the Tree Neutral® program. Tree Neutral offsets the number of trees consumed in the production and printing of this book by taking proactive steps such as planting trees in direct proportion to the number of trees used to print books. To learn more about Tree Neutral, please visit www.treeneutral.com.

TreeNeutral

Since 1917, the Forbes mission has remained constant. Global Champions of Entrepreneurial Capitalism. ForbesBooks exists to further that aim by bringing the Stories, Passion, and Knowledge of top thought leaders to the forefront. ForbesBooks brings you The Best in Business. To be considered for publication, please visit www.forbesbooks.com.

This book is dedicated to the people who have the tenacity and sheer belief that their destiny is theirs to decide. It's my sincere hope that others will join the rest of us and deal their own destiny. Use this book as a guide to go out and do so fearlessly.

TABLE OF CONTENTS

FOREWORD

I t is a great pleasure to tell you about Kate Delaney. Kate and I did a sports talk show on KUHL in Santa Maria, California in the late 90s. I had heard Kate on a local radio show in San Luis Obispo and called her to see if she would be interested in doing a show with me. Fortunately for me she said yes! I found out later she was a television anchor/reporter and was just filling in on the radio, so I was lucky to have heard her.

Kate knew a few sports really well like tennis and hockey, but she was a fast learner and soon picked up on all of the major sports. She always worked with a good question, and a great smile. No matter who we interviewed, she dug deep, did the research, and made it all so interesting. We had some of the biggest names in the sports world on the show. KUHL was a small-market station but the show had a big-market sound.

Kate was, and is, an exceptional talent. In a world dominated by male talk show hosts, she not only broke the glass ceiling; she shattered it. It is one thing to open the door for someone you think is talented, it is quite another to watch them take the opportunity and make a professional career from it. Kate did this through hard work and her love of the business.

You will learn a lot about Kate in this book. I hope you are able to pick up what drives her and has made her a success in all of the areas she has chosen to work.

Kate is an inspiration to all women and men working to have a successful career in their chosen field.

—Roger Blaemire

ACKNOWLEDGMENTS

There is no way I could be living and dealing my own destiny without my mother, Kathleen Delaney's, influence. She made a difference in every life she touched—especially mine. Mom always encouraged me to do what I wanted to do even if everyone else had a different plan, including her.

To my amazing husband, Paul, for his unconditional support on this crazy journey. To my unbelievably talented nephew, Owen, for already realizing it's okay to pursue your own destiny. To Patrick and Crissy Delaney, who are always there for me. Thanks to Aunt Nancy for her support and love that sustains me and thanks to my mother-in-law, Cheryl Jennings, for always being there for us.

There are so many people that helped and encouraged me on my broadcast path both in television and radio. Long-time Philadelphia television personality, Carol Erickson, helped me straight out of college with television footage and a job as a production assistant at KYW.

Others in television include all of the special photographers I worked with including John Montgomery, who always made me look good, and countless editors and producers including Don Sattler, who gave the best tip ever: "Write like you talk, you're funny!" My two favorite TV news directors and the two who encouraged and mentored me the most: Ralph Green and Dan Webster.

To the so many wonderful producers who are like the glue at KRLD such as Ashley Ernisse. Thanks to Spence Kendrick who brought me to Dallas for a slot on KTCK in Dallas, a life changing experience for me. Mark Chernoff, who hired at WFAN in New York City and all the crew who also supported me on air. All of the technical people and fabulous producers at the NBC Sports Radio Network and Jack Silver, the program director for his belief.

Thanks to my National Speakers Association family in Dallas and across the country. I don't want to leave anyone out but you all know who you are! The fantastic meeting planners and audiences I have the privilege of working with from all of sorts of venues, oh what fun we have! To my consulting clients who trust me with their business as we continue thrive together.

To my motley crew of friends: thanks to Annie Zidarevich and Kris Depowski for always being there for me. I'd also like to thank Jill Schiefelbein, Mika Teachout, Christine Cashen, Nikki Nanos, Meridith Elliot-Powell, Shawna Suckow, Ruby Newell-Legner, Pilar Ortiz, Anna Liotta, Dave Lieber, Michael Hoffman, Delatorro McNeal, Stu Schlackman, Chris Price, Susan Reid, KV, and Mary Lou Davidson. Also, Nathan Reeder and the GCN gang. Thanks also to the dog park girls: Annie Dutton, Jalynn Chabot, Johanna Hinkle, and Gail Wheeler. To Ellen Ratner, Bob Ney, and Justin Duckham from Talk Media News, thanks for all of your support.

Last but not least, thanks to the amazing team at Advantage|ForbesBooks: Eland Mann and the whole editorial team; Kristin Hackler, the best shadow ever; Saara Khalil; Gregg Stebben; Melanie Cloth; and Rusty Shelton. Big thanks to the king of Authority Marketing, Adam Witty, the founder and CEO of Advantage|ForbesBooks.

INSIDE THE
LOCKER ROOM

know I'm not the first woman to ever walk into a professional locker room. Most of you reading this book have probably been in the locker room at a gym or during high school, but have you ever been in a professional one? If so, what about one with seventy naked guys in it?

For me, it was like walking into a fully loaded man cave without a bar. The decor featured TVs mounted up high, wall-to-wall lockers, and a very plush, very blue carpet. The first thing I noticed was that the guys were all in various stages of undress; some were dripping wet and just had towels wrapped around their waists. My own hands were soaked with sweat, and I'm the kind of person who never perspires. That was my first foray into the locker room, and it was also the day I really learned to Look Up.

All eyes were on me when I walked in. And before I could say a word, I dropped my microphone. You could have heard a pin drop. To look down at where I'd dropped the microphone was to, well, look down. I'd just about steeled myself to do it when I heard the pad of naked footsteps next to me. Suddenly one of the players was in front of me, handing me the mike—sans towel for all I knew because I wouldn't look down—and smiling.

"Darling," he said to me, "We sure are glad you're here."

Since that day, I've invaded no less than 780 professional locker rooms. Getting to that point—where I had enough clout to walk into a professional sports team's locker room and be taken seriously—was no easy feat. It took 500 rejections to even crack that door.

In *Deal Your Own Destiny,* you'll discover how to stack the cards in your favor as you witness the tenacity, the belief, and the sheer determination it took in my case to break through enormous obstacles to make it in the male-dominated sports radio world, and you'll see how, along the way, I realized I wasn't alone. You'll also find out what I uncovered through 16,000 interviews with rock stars from the C-suite, successful entrepreneurs, Hall of Fame athletes, and others on what it takes to deal your own destiny.

In the beginning of my career, I was pretty much alone in my field as a female national radio sportscaster. It took a lot of self-belief, as well as the support and belief of others, to reach where I am today, and I'm still climbing that ladder, shattering newer and higher ceilings as I go. It wasn't—and still isn't—an easy climb, but along the way I found that there were several basic principles that, time and again, came back to assist me in my pursuits, and it's these principles that I look forward to sharing with you in this book.

Through the sheer strength of believing in ourselves and the power of dedication, teamwork, life balance, and knowing who we are, I've found that each and every one of us is capable of becoming extraordinary. At the end of each chapter you'll find a set of "Play-makers" stories—people I've interviewed or met throughout the course of my career who I feel have exemplified the principle I speak to in each chapter. Then, for those of you who like to jump right in and take action, there's a series of "Curveball" questions to get you thinking and acting. Because you can read about the "how" all day—

it's when you actively take the steps toward dealing your destiny that you actually begin to embrace your extraordinary you.

CHAPTER 1

COME OUT SWINGING: BELIEVING IN YOURSELF

Some people say I have an attitude—maybe I do, but I think you have to. You have to believe in yourself when no one else does—that makes you a winner right there.

VENUS WILLIAMS

I was five years old and living in Queens, New York, when my dad took me to my first ball game. I remember it vividly—the stadium was so big that I couldn't wrap my mind around it. It was just this looming monolith and inside was a sea of blue—Mets fans were everywhere I looked, which would have been fine … if I wasn't rooting for the Phillies.

Before we even left for the game, I remember my mom talking on the phone with my grandmother, and before she hung up she handed the phone to me.

"I heard you're going to the baseball game," Grandmom said. "And you're going to root for the Phillies, right? Like Grandmom does? They're the red team."

I nodded vigorously. "Yes, Grandmom," I said, smiling.

But then we walked into that stadium and all I saw was blue, blue, blue. Of course I now know those were the Mets fans, but to me at the time, they were the blue guys and the Phillies were the red guys.

As the game got underway, the Mets took the lead and all around me the blue guys were jumping up and down, screaming and cheering and overall excited. Then all of a sudden one of the red guys hit a home run and there was this cloudburst of boos from the crowd. Everyone went from happy to this dark storm of negativity.

And I started to cry. I wanted to cheer so badly because one of the red guys—my team, my Grandmom's team—had hit a home run and I wanted to be excited for them, but I was afraid to because everyone else was booing.

Right then my dad took me in his arms.

"What's wrong, Katie?" he asked.

"The red guys," I said through my tears. "Didn't they do something good? Why did everyone boo?"

He smiled and shook his head.

"Because they're rooting for the other team," he said. Then he looked me in the eyes and said, "But that doesn't mean you can't root for the team that you like. Never feel like you can't do what you want to do, even if other people aren't doing it."

> *Never feel like you can't do what you want to do, even if other people aren't doing it.*

Of course, I could barely process this concept at the age of five, but I knew that a feeling of euphoria came over me. If my dad says it's okay, I thought, then it's okay. I can root for them. I can cheer for my own team, even if everyone else isn't. So I did.

For the rest of the game, I didn't care what the blue guys were doing. I cheered for the red team, the Phillies, and Dad even got me a Phillies cap to wear, which I did, proudly. And I still feel the tap on the bill that these crusty old New Yorkers would give me as they walked by, as though they were proud of me—they didn't agree with me, of course, but they were proud of me for standing up for my team.

It made me feel cool to have that approval. I didn't have to be like everyone else—I could stand up for my team and be proud of them.

I didn't realize how important that moment was in my life until years later, when I started to do speaking tours and an interviewer was pushing me on the question of "What made you think you could do sports as a woman, even though you were constantly being rejected?" And all of a sudden, I remembered that moment. All of my tenacity, my ability to look at where everyone else was going and decide to confidently go in the opposite direction without a second thought, came from that moment—when my dad told me I could be different from everyone else and that there was nothing wrong with that.

As one of the few women doing sports radio on a national level, I've faced my share of obstacles over the years, and along the way I've found that this "deal your own destiny" approach isn't unique to rising stars in the business world—it's also a core value of most successful athletes. This book is partly about the path I followed to where I am today, but it's also about the common barriers that successful entrepreneurs and athletes alike have met and conquered. This is my story, a story of patience, determination, and believing wholeheartedly in oneself.

DRAFTED

It wasn't my lifelong goal to become the first woman with a national sports radio talk show. It became my goal, but I didn't start out with it.

One of my first "career" jobs was as a television reporter/anchorwoman for KSBY in San Luis Obispo, California. I was working with John Whelehan, who was the station's weekend sportscaster, and one day John asked if I would be willing to fill in for him.

"You know as much about sports as I do," he said. "I have a vacation coming up, and while I'm out you should fill in for me."

And that was that. He talked to the news director about it, and before I knew it I was scheduled to fill in for him.

At first I panicked. I was just building up a good reputation as a news anchor, and there were hardly any women doing sports news. What if I messed up? What if I ruined my news career before it began?

But in the back of my mind was a sense of elation. This was a huge opportunity, and I knew it was something I wanted to do. So I took the leap and filled in—and it was great. In fact, by the time John came back, the news director said that while they didn't have any sportscasting openings at the time, she'd consider me in a heartbeat if they did.

Being a sportscaster fueled me, buoyed me up, because I knew I was on the right path. I wanted to become a sportscaster and nothing was going to stand in my way.

"If you're tuning in for the first time, we have Kate Delaney with us all week joining our morning team on KUHL."

Not long after my stint as a television newscaster, I had the opportunity to fill in at a local radio station doing sports (actually, I was doing other reporting as well, but sports was part of it). What I didn't know at the time was that the station was being sold to a man named Roger Blaemire, the former VP for business operations for the Cincinnati Reds, who happened to hear one of my sports reports while he was driving from Los Angeles through the Central Coast.

A few days later I got a call from him out of the blue.

"I want to talk to you about working for me," he said, barely taking the time to introduce himself before getting to the point. "I want you to do an hour-long, drive-time sports talk show."

Just that thought was daunting. Are you kidding me? I was thinking sports casts. Sports casts are a minute long, but a whole hour? "I'm not sure, I can do sixty minutes," I said.

Roger shot back immediately, "I bet you could fill six hours." In my heart and my head, I was already fueled up. I knew I could do it. But I was also skeptical. Just because someone tells you you're great and that they're interested in hiring you doesn't mean it's a done deal. And the next words out of his mouth confirmed that thought.

"Just be patient," he said. "I'm buying this station, but the process takes time and we're still in the beginning stages."

Two months later and nothing had happened. Three months later and I'd pretty much put the idea of doing a sports talk show for Roger out of my head. I continued to send my tape and resume out to other stations, and four months after our talk, just about when I had given up on it, Roger called me up and asked me to come talk to him about the show.

I went to his office, and the next thing I knew I had my first talk show—an hour-long sports program.

HERE I AM

Roger ended up becoming a good friend and mentor. Just from those short sports updates he heard me giving for the station, he could tell that I was capable of filling an hour. Even I didn't know I could do it. I mean, how do you go from doing a couple minute updates to a whole sports talk show?

Fortunately, he understood what a big leap this was and did the shows with me in the beginning. As we were brainstorming what we would do, he said, "Make a wish list of the people you want to get on the show. No holds barred." Of all the people in the world of sports, who would I most like to talk to?

And pretty much every person I put on the list, Roger got on the show. We had some of the biggest names in sports at that time on the show, because he either knew them or knew how to get ahold of them, and he taught me how to do the same. "Just do it," he said. "Just call them up."

> *Even though I believed in myself and knew that I wanted to do sports, I was still way out of my comfort zone.*

It was a challenge for me, because even though I believed in myself and knew that I wanted to do sports, I was still way out of my comfort zone. But I followed his lead and found myself at the beginning of my real career. There I was on the radio, talking sports and letting the world know that "Here I am."

ALL THE STATS

In those very early days, I felt like I needed to know everything there was to know about sports. I knew a lot, but I thought I needed to know it all—World Series stats from the 1940s and 1950s, and details that I was far too young to know and yet wanted to be prepared for in case someone brought them up on the show. So I bought the ESPN encyclopedia, which gives you the history of just about every sport, and all these reference books that did a deeper dive into all of the details. I was ready for anything. Then one day a guest on the show said to me, off air, "You are so good, you don't need these books." And he threw them in the trash. There must have been four or five of them stacked on my desk, and he swiped them all into the bin at once.

"These facts," he said, waving his hand at the overturned books, "they don't matter. You can't know every single thing. You're not an encyclopedia. That's not what sports is all about."

Suddenly it was as though I was five again and my dad was looking me in the eyes and telling me that I didn't have to do what everyone else was doing.

From that moment, I stopped using those books. I stopped worrying about knowing every single detail. Because he was right, I did know a lot about sports, and it's humanly impossible to know everything. That's not what a talk show is about. What it's about is making games come alive—it's about personalities and opinions and so much more than dry statistics from games that ended thirty-five years ago.

The last thing that guest said to me was "Don't doubt yourself." Suddenly it was as though I was five again and my dad was looking me in the eyes and telling me that I didn't have to do what everyone else was doing. I could go my own road and take it as far as I wanted, as long as I believed in myself. It was a poignant reminder and one that's stuck with me ever since.

HOODWINKED IN VEGAS

Doing that show for Roger Blaemire was my first real taste of the sports talk radio world. The station was sort of tucked away on a street in a residential neighborhood. You could almost drive by and not realize live radio was happening up the steps and behind the doors of what looked like an ordinary house. The station wasn't modernized and still used carts (tape cartridges) for capturing and playing sound. However, the race to make the air, the mics, the headphones, the commercials, and the chaos of it all was awesome. What a great time we all had taking a small station in Santa Maria, California, and making radio like we were in Los Angeles.

That was the problem in the end. I knew I wanted more; I wanted to be bigger. I was working for a small radio station in a small town, and as much fun as the show was, I wasn't going anywhere with it. So I started to talk to people, as many as I could track down, and submitted my tape and resume to them.

Eventually I came across this national platform called the Sports Fan Radio Network, which lured me in with the promise of putting me on the air as long as I helped produce and do a few other things. Basically, they hoodwinked me, but I didn't find that out until I'd moved to the network branch in Las Vegas.

It was an easy move. Vegas is pretty close to California, and they offered me a place to live, along with a salary, so it seemed like a great deal. Plus, the show was going to be syndicated; how could I turn that down?

But there was no show for me when I got to Vegas. I ended up working more as a producer, and it turned out that they never really intended to give me a show in the first place. It was a definite step backward and one I didn't know I'd made until I was in the middle of it.

It took some time, but eventually, as they kept re-racking their programming, I ended up cohosting a show—though it was definitely *just* cohosting. And I wasn't the only one getting the runaround on what the job actually entailed. They brought in guys from all over the country, all of them with the same hope as me—to do a nationally syndicated radio show—and what we found was a hefty workload with multiple roles rolled into one, all for a struggling business whose paychecks bounced half the time.

What most of us failed to realize when we signed up with the Sports Fan Radio Network was that we were all jumping into an entrepreneurial pursuit. This was no established company; there were risks involved and there were times when the executives would just ask us to "be patient" with them—that they were "getting funding" or "getting an infusion" soon and *then* we'd get paid.

In the meantime, we were stuck in the middle of the desert, having given up our homes in pursuit of a promise, and finding out that the risk wasn't really panning out.

So to soothe our spirits, we went to Magoo's.

ONE HUNDRED DRINKS AT MAGOO'S

Magoo's was a local sports dive bar right off the main Vegas strip, and it quickly became the place we went to blow off steam.

Even though we were never sure if or when we were going to get paid, very few of us gave up and left. We knew there was going to be some risk involved, but we were in a risky town, so it kind of made sense that we rolled the dice and took our chances.

While we waited for those paychecks to stick and for the opportunity to host a show, we bonded, and we helped each other when we could—and one way we did that was by buying drinks at Magoo's.

Every other Friday—when the network execs did give us a check—it was a mad race to the bank to get our checks cashed before everyone else, because if we waited too long they would probably bounce. If we did make it in time, though, we were buying beer for everyone else.

I still have that mug from Magoo's on my desk—which I had to earn, by the way; you had to punch a hundred drinks on your Magoo's card before they'd give you one—and every day it reminds me of those early struggles and the bonds we built.

WE'VE GOT SPIRIT

Vegas had its moments, but it wasn't a great situation, and after enough Fridays of being told that we were just waiting on that next infusion of cash, I began sending out resumes again. Thanks to the help of an engineer friend of mine, Bill Brown, I was able to put together some decent tapes and just started sending them out to anywhere I could think of, hoping to land a ticket out of this land of money and possibility and madness.

In the midst of it all, I remember coming across a copy of Deepak Chopra's book, *The Seven Spiritual Laws of Success,* and though I'd never been into self-help books, this one really spoke to me. Teachings like the Law of Detachment and the Law of Least Effort made a lot of sense. Ultimately, the book led me to understand that if I practiced non-judgment, believed in myself, and focused on my goals, then I'd be able to achieve those aspirations.

"Stick it out," the book said (I'm paraphrasing, of course). "Don't be the victim. Just keep believing and don't pay attention to the people who tell you to stop trying."

So as I sent out resumes and made new tapes and applied, applied, applied all over the country, I kept reading that book and believing in myself while trying not to focus on all of the negative things that were going on around me.

Then, all of a sudden, I started to get replies—not just one or two here and there, but a lot. I got a call from a network in Atlanta and another one in Houston. A place in Dallas called me up, too, and all were offering me serious positions at decent salaries.

I ended up interviewing with the Dallas network— KTCK Dallas "The Ticket"— since they already carried some of the syndicated programming from Vegas and they also had an incredible contract. They sent it

Then, all of a sudden, I started to get replies— not just one or two here and there, but a lot.

to me before I flew down to interview, and my brother, who'd just graduated from law school, reviewed it for me.

"Oh, this the best deal I've ever seen you get," he said to me after reading it. "Take it!"

It was a real, honest-to-goodness broadcasting contract, with decent pay and bonuses for doing extra work like endorsements, so even though I was looking at some other networks that were interested in me, I signed the contract, packed my bags, and headed for Dallas.

Before I left, though, I did the professional thing and handed in my notice to Sports Fan Radio. Since the network had never been that reliable on paying me every two weeks, I wasn't too concerned about giving them a full two weeks notice when I left. I just went in to the manager, Charlie, and said, "Here's my resignation. I've been hired at a network in Dallas. Thanks, it's been fun."

The first thing he said to me was "Wow. Who are you cohosting for?"

When I told him it was my own show, he was shocked. He couldn't get it through his head that not only did this huge radio station in Dallas want me, they were giving me a prime spot under my own name—*The Kate Delaney Show* during the evening drive from 7 to 10 p.m.

PLAYMAKERS: TOM BRADY

There can't be enough said about the value of believing in yourself. Take Tom Brady, arguably one of the best NFL quarterbacks in history. He was picked sixth in the draft and was backup quarterback for Drew Bledsoe until Bledsoe got hurt and Brady stepped in. The rest, of course, is history—at forty years old, Tom had appeared in eight Super Bowls and won five of them.

Before that, however, he'd never really stood out. At Serra High School in San Mateo, California, Tom started out on the football team as backup, only playing when someone got hurt. His junior year, he made starter on varsity, but he still wasn't making many waves, particularly with the colleges he was applying to. By the end of his junior year, Tom's dad decided to take matters into his own hands and helped his son do some marketing. Together they created a highlights reel of his past season, including a recommendation from his coach, Tom McKenzie, and sent it out to fifty-four colleges. It was this tape that led to Michigan assistant coach Bill Harris getting in touch with Tom Brady and his family, and ultimately led to Tom attending and playing for Michigan.

Still, Tom had a hard time standing out. He was seventh-string quarterback until his junior season, when he had to battle freshman rising star Drew Henson for time on the field. The arrangement lasted into Tom's senior year, with Tom replacing Henson if Henson messed up and vice versa in a tactic called platooning quarterbacks. This led to Tom recovering several games that Henson started, bringing his team to comeback victories against Notre Dame, Ohio State, Penn State, and Alabama.

In sports, just as in business, you can't just wish for something to happen.

Even with such an incredible season under his belt, Tom still couldn't catch a break. In the 2000 NFL draft, he wasn't picked until the sixth round and was the 199th selection overall, which was humiliating for him. It wasn't until that next year, 2001, when Drew Bledsoe was injured, that Brady stepped in and the rest is NFL history.

There were so many opportunities for Tom to quit. He dealt with depression in college and almost switched to Cal-Berkeley when he didn't feel like he was making any headway at Michigan, but he stuck with it because deep down he had a massive belief in himself. He knew that he was good enough, and because of that, he trained with unrelenting focus. Instead of letting himself go a little in the off-season like most football players, Tom wouldn't even look at a pizza. He worked out obsessively and was disciplined to the extreme. He knew that if he was going to get to where he wanted to be, he needed to dedicate himself to it fully. So he did, and he made it.

In sports, just as in business, you can't just wish for something to happen. There's no genie who appears and grants you the break you need to make it big. You need the skills and you have to develop them unrelentingly, and you have to be ready for the opportunity when and if it arises.

That discipline is one of the hardest things to maintain. To "deal your own destiny," you must believe in yourself on a grand scale, but you also need to have the discipline to learn, to do, and to strive.

A lot of people probably told Tom Brady to give up on the football thing. He's a smart guy—they probably told him to let the idea of making it big in sports and go and become, a coach, a teacher, or businessman.

> *You must believe in yourself on a grand scale, but you also need to have the discipline to learn, to do, and to strive.*

I was told the same thing. "You're smart," people would say. "Why don't you become an investment banker or a lawyer? Why are you pursuing sports radio?" Even the people I worked with in Vegas would ask why I didn't just give up. "Go deal baccarat," one guy told me. "You'd make a fortune with your personality."

But that wasn't my dream. I knew what I wanted to be, and I pursued it relentlessly. Even in the face of torrential rejection.

CURVEBALLS

What self-limiting beliefs are holding you back? Really dig deep and think about this question. Trust me, we all have them, but recognizing them is the first step. Write them down and start to tackle those SLBs.

Are you afraid to fail? It is easy to get complacent. Surround yourself with mementos of past successes. Some people I know even have these in a box on their desk. Look at, say, a trophy you won and remember what it took to get it.

Is asking for what you want too tough because you are afraid of rejection? This too is something to work on and often is a self-limiting belief. What's the worst that can happen? If you don't step forward, you will always be in the same place. If you don't ask the answer is always no. Increase your odds of success by working on ditching those negative thoughts of rejection.

Are you worrying about being your true authentic self for fear of being judged? Surround yourself with people who love you for you. Get rid of the people telling you how you should act and feel.

Do you believe that what you have to offer just isn't good enough? If your answer is yes, do some more research, dig deeper again, and refine your offer. What makes you unique?

Focus on that, and you'll come up with something you feel more confident about offering.

CHAPTER 2

FIRE UP YOUR FAN BASE: GETTING OTHERS TO BELIEVE IN YOU

To be a great champion, you must believe you are the best. If you're not, pretend that you are.

MUHAMMAD ALI

If you don't believe you'll succeed, you won't. It's a hard thing to do some days, and early in your career it's hard to do most days, but you can't let the opposition hold you back—even if that opposition is just your own fears. You're always the furthest away from your goal at the start, but you get closer to it with every step. And the more you believe in yourself, the more others sense that belief, and over time they start to believe in you, too—and that's where you really start to build momentum. Once you have a fan base, you know you're on a roll.

IN THE FACE OF REJECTION

The offer from KTCK Dallas was huge, but it wasn't a quick win. I had to steel myself against a seemingly endless stream of no's before landing The Ticket out of Vegas.

Before The Ticket offer, I was ready, in a way, for more rejection letters. I knew that not every radio and television station in the country would be falling all over themselves for a female sportscaster, and I'd applied to just about all of them. I actually had this big map of the United States, and every chance I got I would look at it and think, "Okay, where could I make a decent living?" Then I'd circle it and apply to the stations in that area, calling each of them up to find out who was in charge and sending them my television and radio tapes along with my resume.

Then, a week or so later, the rejection letters would start to come in. From Bakersfield, California, to Sarasota, Florida, I got letters saying "We filled the position," or "We're not interested," or I wouldn't hear anything at all.

A ROCKY INTERVIEW

On one occasion, I actually got a callback from a TV station in Bozeman, Montana—a small town in the Rocky Mountains that's also home to Montana State University and the MSU Bobcats. I didn't even stop to think about whether or not I, a city girl born and raised in Philly, would be happy living in a small college town. It was a chance at an opportunity and I took it.

Thinking back on it, however, I recall that I had a bad feeling about that interview before I even walked in the front door.

The station offered to fly me out, and when I arrived the first thing they asked me to do was take a test to see how much I knew about sports. Now, I wasn't a seasoned veteran of sports radio at that point, but I also wasn't a spring chicken. I'd built up a pretty good reputation, with the resume to prove it, and for some station manager to ask me to take a test was crazy insulting.

I was so appalled by the test that to this day I'm still surprised I didn't just ball it up and throw it in his face, and demand to be driven back to the airport. Instead I took it, answered all fifty-or-so questions, and handed it in, all the while thinking that coming to this interview had been a terrible idea.

They had me do an on-air segment after the test, too, which was fine, but by the time I was done I knew that the interview had been a complete waste of time. The whole situation stank of someone just checking off a box on their EOE obligations, and I went home without any hope—or desire—to hear back from them.

"WOMEN DON'T BELONG IN THE LOCKER ROOM"

I won't say who the epitome of all my rejection letters came from, because every time I share his letter with other women, they get the same murderous look in their eyes that I did the first time I read it. All I'll say is that this came from a small station in a small town, and it read:

> *Dear Kate,*
> *Thank you for the tape your work is good. I have a strong suspicion that a woman would struggle in this role. Sports really is a man's domain. Women are more suited to morning shows and fun, easy-breezy features.*
> *Good luck,*
> *John*

That was it. When I read that letter, I knew there was no turning back. There was no investment banker or lawyer future for me. I was going to break into the sports talk radio world in a big way, and nothing was going to stand in my way.

HOW 'BOUT THEM COWBOYS?

I'd only been at The Ticket for a couple of days when someone asked if I wanted the network's seat on the Cowboys charter to their upcoming game against the Eagles in my hometown.

"You can grab some tape and bring it back after the game," he said, and of course, I was all in. But he didn't give me a lot of details. It was an interesting thing, trying to get on that Cowboys plane and fly to Philly.

I found the jet in a private loading area on the back side of the airport, and it was clear from the beginning that I had no idea what I was doing. I tried to load my giant piece of luggage on my own, find my seat, and figure out what I was supposed to be doing, but instead of asking for help, I just tried to figure it out on my own. That was a mistake. If I'd asked, "What should I know about traveling on the Cowboys charter?" before I left, I wouldn't have felt so embarrassed by having more gear than the guys playing the game. I also would have been earlier and wouldn't have raced up the staircase to the plane like I had just completed the forty-yard dash. I almost missed the plane and that wouldn't have been good for the station or me. Only a few radio stations were given a free seat on the charter. Not showing up could mean the team pulls your seat.

Instead, there I was, not asking questions and pretending to look like I knew what was up, getting onto a private charter jet with a roster that included heavy hitter names like Troy Aikman and Emmitt Smith. Somehow, I managed it. I finally found my seat, and just as I settled in someone handed me what looked like a duffel bag full of food with the Cowboys' star on the side. Inside it was like Willy Wonka land. There was a giant sub and these Kit Kat bars that could have been pontoons for a seaplane. If I'd eaten everything in it, I would have gained twenty pounds, easily.

"You've got to be kidding me," I said to myself as I dug through all the goodies.

One of the players walking by just then must have overheard me, because he stopped and said, "You're a rookie. You see those guys behind you? If you don't want it, pass it back, because this is just the appetizer. The meal is coming up next."

Finally, the plane landed and we loaded onto buses for the final leg of the journey. Even though there wasn't so much as a blue star logo identifying us, somehow there were Cowboy fans along the route, cheering the entourage as it went by. By the time we got to the hotel, the smattering of fans had become a mob, and for a moment

I understood what it must be like to be a rock star. We could barely get off of the buses with all the fans waving and yelling and holding signs as we walked by.

As it got to be my turn to climb down into the sea of fans, I suddenly caught a glimpse of my mom at the very back of the crowd, waiting to pick me up and take me home. I tried a couple of times to force my way toward her, but the fans weren't budging. Then all of sudden I heard someone say, "Get out of the way!"

It was Nate Newton, one of the Cowboys' giant linemen, and he was forcing his way through the crowd in front of me, parting them like the Red Sea and pulling me along behind him. When we reached my mom, he swooped his arms around her, gave her this big bear hug, and said, "Hi, mom!"

The shock on my mother's face was priceless. She's always been this pretty, elegant little lady, and there she was, standing at the edge of a fan-crazy crowd in her heels and suit, with the arms of this enormous football player wrapped around her.

The whole trip felt like a comedy of errors, but I made it to Philly, I got to see the game, and I got some great tape afterward. And I wouldn't have been there if the crew at The Ticket hadn't believed in me.

PERSONAL BRANDING: PRINCESSES AREN'T LEPRECHAUNS

Getting people to believe that you can do the job you want and do it well is tough. It's tough in any industry, no matter what you do, because in order to earn that belief you have to sell yourself. Just think about the last time you were at a job interview for a position you really wanted. You knew you could do it and that you would be great at it, but you were up against however many other candidates who wanted the job just as much. How did you sell yourself? What did you think made you unique? What helped you and what hurt you?

The answer to those questions is the foundation of personal branding: those things about you that leave an impression with others. We're constantly doing things to help our personal branding or hurt it, and a lot of the things that end up hurting it start out as a good idea. For me, that's where the leprechaun came in.

It sounded like a good idea at first—a quick way to make $3,000 at a time when paying the rent was still a personal achievement every month. All I had to do was dress up like a leprechaun on St. Patrick's Day and pass out cupcakes at a company party. I was all ready to do it, too, when I started to think about how that gig could hurt my personal brand. I was just starting to break into my own in sportscasting, and while I didn't mind being a little goofy on air, pictures of me dressed as a leprechaun could seriously damage my reputation. Was it worth $3,000 to take a hit like that?

No, it wasn't, but in really considering how taking a well-paying gig could hurt my personal brand, I starting thinking about my personal brand in serious terms. What about me stood out? How could I leverage those things that made me unique?

When I was still getting my chops as a host, I had a caller on the air who went back and forth with me on a couple of interesting stats before saying, "You know what? You're like the Princess of Sports. Don't ever say 'I think' anymore. You're good, you know this stuff."

After that call, people at the network and even callers started calling me the Sports Princess, and the name just stuck. In fact, I ended up trademarking it, and even though I don't use it as much today, the name "Sports Princess" is one of the most important and, early on, most influential parts of my personal branding.

FROM DALLAS TO SEATTLE—BY BICYCLE

Then there are the personal branding decisions that take everything you have to make them happen but end up paying out big time down the road. It could be waking up every morning at 4:00 a.m. for a year to build and promote your website or staying up after everyone's gone to sleep to finish a project by a promised time. It's exhausting, but it's an immediate reflection of who you are.

I run into personal branding decisions constantly in the course of my job, and one of the decisions I made early on is now a part of who I am for the rest of my life—the day I agreed to ride my bike from Dallas to Seattle if the Rangers lost to the Mariners.

At that point in my career, my contract with the Dallas network that had delivered me from Vegas was up, and the big Texas Ranger network on the other side of town—KRLD—had offered me a job: sports director with a regular talk show. KRLD was a much bigger network and one step closer to my goal, so I took the job, and not long after that I was deep in a brainstorming session with the network directors, trying to answer the big question: How can we get more people excited about the Rangers when they're having a really poor season?

We bounced around several ideas, including one that I immediately put the kibosh on, which was riding a roller coaster for twenty-four hours if the Rangers lost (this idea only came up because the Rangers ballpark is located right next to Six Flags Texas). Finally, we settled on the idea of me placing an on-air bet with the audience—if the Rangers lost, then I would ride my bike to the city of whichever team beat them. It seemed like a safe bet at the time. Even if the Rangers lost, most of the cities in the American League West were pretty close by. There were only a few outliers, like Seattle, and of course it was Seattle that ended up winning the division.

There are 2,000 miles between Dallas and Seattle. It would have been a tough ride even if I had been a cyclist, but I didn't cycle at all. The network got a trainer to work with me, and they even built me a bike that said "Sports Princess" on the side. Fortunately for me, we found a way around the bet that allowed me to honor it while not killing myself riding two thousand-plus miles cross-country. As part of the "bike tour" we had a truck painted with the words "Kate Delaney" and my show hours, along with a caricature of me, and we mounted the bike on the inside of the truck. That way I "rode" from Dallas to Seattle, giving little updates on the journey every day.

I didn't realize how much of an impact that bike ride had until I came back and my hairstylist was telling me how glued everyone had been to the radio.

"Everyone was listening to you," he said. "Everyone in Dallas was talking about it, trying to figure out where you were and where the bike was and what was happening."

In that moment I realized how much of a reach I could have and how much of an impact I could make.

But that wasn't the last time I had to work to get others to believe in me. Not by far.

INSIDER BASEBALL

Even though the gig in Dallas was a good one, I always had my ears open for the next step up the ladder, and one day a friend of mine came to me with some good insider news.

A big broadcasting company on the West Coast was planning on starting a new radio network, and while they hadn't announced yet that they were looking for talent, they would be soon enough. On top of that, the general manager used to live in Dallas and had likely heard some of my work, so I thought I might already have an "in."

I immediately called the GM, who confirmed that the network was hiring and that he'd heard me before and liked my work. He asked me to send in some of my tapes so that he could review them with the team, which I did immediately after the call.

Fast-forward a few weeks and another friend of mine got hired as the assistant program manager at that same network, which boosted my hopes even more … only to be dashed a few days later when she told me about their first talent selection meeting.

She and the GM, whom I'd spoken with earlier, walked into a meeting with the network's program director to start narrowing down the options for on-air talent. My name, she said, was on the board along with a short list of people for the same position. As they got to that section, both she and the program director talked me up to the GM, pointing out that I had good ratings despite being up against more famous personalities in a male-dominated market.

"Oh, I know who Kate is," the GM said when they were done. "I know people like listening to her, but number one, I hate women doing radio, and number two, I definitely hate women doing sports. Erase her name."

> Number one, I hate women doing radio, and number two, I definitely hate women doing sports. Erase her name.

I couldn't believe it, but both the program director and the assistant program director confirmed the story.

Most things in life are subjective, and even when you're successful at what you do and have a great track record, it still doesn't mean you're safe from rejection. I felt that I was certainly qualified for that job, that I was likable and had the ratings to prove it, but because of one guy's prejudice, there was no way I was getting it. To me, that's one of the worst kinds of rejection because there's absolutely nothing you can do about it.

SPORTS JEOPARDY

I knew I was an anomaly in the sports world, but to me that was just another factor that made me stand out. I had a personal brand to build, and what I needed to do was drill down on the things I did well, those things that made me unique.

When I first got into radio, I began doing an exercise that I still do today. I'd draw one line down the center of a sheet of paper and another line across, creating four quadrants. In the first quadrant I'd write down what I was doing, in the second quadrant what I wasn't leveraging, and in the third what made me unique. Then, in the fourth quadrant, I'd list any ideas that came to me, whether it was talking points I hadn't considered, sports figures I hadn't spoken with, or new show ideas. These were my "buzz-worthy" ideas—creative, clever branding concepts that I knew would make me stand out as a top-notch sportscaster, regardless of gender.

One of those ideas that turned out to be wildly popular was a thing I called "Sports Jeopardy."

I held it every Tuesday night for an hour, and people from all over would call in to compete. I had several categories and would research tons of sports questions for each one—nothing too easy, either, as the grand prize was a satellite dish and the full football season package.

Being in Dallas, I of course got on a Cowboys trivia kick now and then, which I really didn't think anything about until one day I received a very brief note in the mail.

"Dear Kate," it read. "Thanks. Barry Switzer."

Now, Barry Switzer was the coach of the Cowboys at the time—a controversial one because he'd formerly been the coach for Oklahoma and he took the place of the Cowboys' very popular previous coach, Jimmy Johnson, but regardless of how Texans felt about him, he was a well-known sports figure. And here he was, not only listening to my show but taking the time to send me a note and say "thanks."

You don't often think about who may be listening to you while you're doing a show. You're insulated in the studio, with your headsets on and your focus split between what you need to do right now and what you need to do immediately afterward. You're not really thinking, "Maybe the mayor's listening to me" or some other famous personality. Until you meet people and they say they've heard your show, you don't really realize how big your audience is.

When I got that note from Switzer, I suddenly realized that there were a lot more people listening to me than I thought, and not only were they listening, but they were enjoying the show.

I did the Sports Jeopardy bit for a while, taking care not to keep it going too long because I didn't want it to get stale, and eventually I switched it out for a "mystery guest" segment in which I'd have someone famous call in—like Kenny Albert, the voice of the New York Rangers—and have people call in and guess who he or she was.

These were all part of my brand, those things I did that made me stand out, and in having these unique angles, I was building my tribe.

NUMBER ONE FAN

What are you doing to fire up your fan base? Are you building your Twitter followers, getting people to listen to your podcast? How do you find those people who really want to hear your ideas? You do it by taking what's unique about you and making it as big as possible— it's about personal branding: leveraging those qualities that set you apart and consistently giving yourself the space to think about how you can stand out even more. And don't be afraid to ask other people! They can be your best resource, because it can be so easy to only see what's in front of you.

That note from Barry Switzer resonated with me. Sure, the phone lines were always jammed with callers when we did the Sports Jeopardy show, but that note drove it home to me that the show was working—I was standing out, not because I was a woman or because I knew my stuff, but because I was engaging and people wanted to be a part of that.

I also had to realize that I wasn't just a statistical machine, spouting out scores and sports facts. I was an entertainer. I had to go against the grain and believe that when I leapt into doing something different—something unconventional—I would succeed. There's a lot of faith—and a lot of fear—in building a powerful personal brand, but if you believe strongly in yourself then others will sense that and get on board. If you want to win big, you have to trust your instincts and often that means doing something different from everyone else.

> *I had to go against the grain and believe that when I leapt into doing something different— something unconventional—I would succeed.*

There were times in my life, here and there, when I thought about dropping the whole pursuit of becoming a national sportscaster and settling for a more secure life. But security is just a mirage. No one is completely secure, and there's an amazing difference when you're building and doing and pursuing, zigzagging and leaping to try and get that one break that you're really looking for and finally being able to do what, deep down, you've always been the most passionate about.

I always found a way to back to the mic and sports radio in some form, even after leaving The Ticket. Whether it was another big opportunity across town in Dallas with KRLD, the station that broadcasted the Texas Rangers baseball games, or a leap back east to WFAN. Weary of not getting big-enough contracts and life changes led to periods of doing something else to make more money.

It was amazing to be back in the saddle again when *The Kate Delaney Show* began airing on NBC in 2015. I was thrilled to be working with an incredibly encouraging program director and a bunch of really supportive guys on the roster; which is important because, just as you can have a great idea and no one to listen to it, you also need an exceptional team to make great things happen. I've been in situations where no one believed in me and I couldn't convince them otherwise. But when they do support you and you have a team that believes in you and your goal, that's when you really start to make things happen. That's when you really begin to shine.

PLAYMAKERS: ERIN ANDREWS, MARK EATON, KEN DANEYKO

Erin Andrews became a big name in sportscasting in the 2000s, but when she was just starting out, her father, who is a sportscaster for an NBC affiliate in Tampa, Florida, tried his best to convince her not to follow that path. His dissuasive attitude was just one of the obstacles Erin faced, but when I asked her about those kinds of challenges, she said that she'd never thought of doing anything else.

"This [being a sports talk show host] is kind of all I've ever talked about doing," Erin explained to me during an interview. "I didn't even have a backup plan, because it was my passion and I believed I was going to do it."

Eventually, Erin won her dad over and he became an amazing resource for her.

"My dad and I would text each other back and forth during games," Erin said. "He'd tell me to slow down and take a breath, or I would text him and ask him things like 'Dad, what am I going to ask Mike McCarthy?' after they [the Packers] lost in Atlanta for the NFC Championship."

One of Erin's favorite moments so far in her career, in fact, happened when her dad was at a Red Sox game with her. It was right after the Boston bombing occurred, and the Red Sox had just won the game.

"My dad was there on the field with me," she said, "and we were walking back to the clubhouse when Big Papi, one of my favorite players ever, came out and started spraying champagne on us and everywhere. It was a really special moment."

For Erin, it didn't matter what anyone else thought about her being a woman in the sports talk show world. She knew it was the career she wanted and she knew that she could do it, regardless of the challenges.

Mark Eaton is another person who believed in himself even when others didn't—and stuck with pursuing his goal until he changed everyone's minds.

In the late 1970s, Mark was a mechanic who dreamed of playing basketball. He transferred to UCLA to play, but in his first two years with the Bruins he only logged about forty-two minutes on the court. He was frustrated, and despite his height advantage (he was 7'4" without shoes on), people told him to forget about ever playing basketball professionally.

But he didn't give up, and in 1982 he found his niche just in time to be drafted seventy-second by the NBA.

So how was he able to go from auto mechanic to NBA player, apart from sheer tenacity and drive? A lot of it, Mark said to me while we were attending a Sports Celebrity workshop, was thanks to his mentors.

"Who was your greatest mentor?" I asked him.

"That's an easy one, Kate," he said. "Wilt Chamberlain."

While he was at UCLA, Mark explained, Wilt told him he was running around all over the place and that he just needed to stop and focus on one thing. What was that one thing?

"Play defense and park under the basket," Wilt told Mark. That was the lightbulb Mark needed—from that day on, he approached the game exactly that way, making it his job to protect the basket.

For eleven years, Mark played for the Utah Jazz and quickly became one of the best defensive players in basketball history. His defense helped the Jazz make their first ever appearance in the playoffs, and over the course of his career he earned two NBA Defensive Player of the Year awards and held the NBA record for most blocks in a season (456), with a career average of 3.5 blocked shots per game. In 1995, the Jazz retired his number, fifty-three, for the many contributions he made to the team.

"Mr. Devil" Ken Daneyko also never stood down from his dream. During an interview, he told me how hockey was a part of his life for as long as he could remember. From the age of seven on, he told his mother almost every day, "I'm going to play in the National Hockey League."

"And my mother knew that only a small percentage of hockey players ever made it to the NHL, so she would pacify me and say, 'Yeah, yeah, Kenny,' but I'm not sure if she ever believed it," Ken said.

"Then the day came when I played my first game with the NHL in Madison Square Garden. I was nineteen years old, and my mother, who was this little lady barely over five feet tall and who didn't care much for big cities, came out to watch me. Afterward, I remember her saying, 'I don't care if he ever plays another game. He did what he said he was going to do. If he didn't tell me a hundred times a day that he was going to play for the NHL ...' It was just gratifying, for me and for her, when I finally played that game. I went on to play 1,200-plus games and win Stanley Cups, but that first game meant the world to both of us.

"I was fortunate. I played in a great organization and never had to play anywhere else. And I was happy just to get the opportunity to play as long as I did. I worked hard and I wasn't the most skilled player on the team, but I brought an element that the team needed, and to play twenty years and all the games I did—that was what it was all about."

Even when people start to believe in you, it's hard not to feel underestimated. I never knew what those network managers were thinking when they passed on me. Was it because I wasn't good or because they just didn't like the idea of women in the sports world? If I could just get in front of them, I thought, I could prove myself.

I had to toughen myself mentally, especially in those early days when I didn't have many encouragers at all. Over and over I would hear questions like "Why do you deal with this? Why do you put up with people belittling you?" I could have let all those rejection letters discourage me, but I chose not to look at it that way. I was just doing what I loved, having fun, and trying to do some clever things on the radio. I didn't live every day with the thought of "Yeah, I really am an anomaly" in my head. Instead, I felt like the girl who pops out of the cake—no one expects anything when suddenly, "Surprise!" here I am—and I'm fantastic.

CURVEBALLS

Are you surrounding yourself with people who support you or tear you down?

How do you deal with discouragers?

How are you building your tribe?

Do you have a vision board, favorite quotes, or a wall with a few past successes to look at where you can see it easily and often?

CHAPTER 3

LINE DRIVE: DEDICATING YOURSELF TO YOUR PATH

The difference between the impossible and the possible lies in a person's determination.

TOMMY LASORDA

I f you've ever seen *Wild*, the movie adapted from a book of the same name, then you probably remember the part of the movie where Reese Witherspoon's character—the book's author, Cheryl Strayed—is picked up by a truck driver who asks her, more or less, "What kind of a woman are you?" Cheryl goes on to share some of her regrets about the choices she's made in her life, and then asks the driver if he's ever had any forks in his road.

"Never been a time in my life when there's a fork in my road," he replies.

She thinks about that for a moment, then says, "There's been nothing but forks in mine."

I think of that scene often when I think about my own life path. There have been a lot of forks in my road and many places where I could have jumped off … and at least a few places where I almost did.

How many times have you been asked about your path? It's almost as if not having one is unacceptable. I thought the forks were bad until I realized that it's about the journey. Not only did my journey become my path, I also found that when you dedicate yourself to your path, you find that the detours along the way seem a whole lot less scary.

THE KICKOFF

Growing up, my mom wanted my brother and I to be as open-minded as possible, so she exposed us to as much culture as she could. One week we might be at the American Ballet Theatre watching *The Nut-cracker*, the next in the middle of a hardcore hockey crowd cheering for the Philadelphia Flyers.

I have nothing against ballet, but I loved the raw excitement of those hockey games, even as a kid. We'd go to the arena and you could just feel it in the air—that excited anticipation before the game, the passion during it, and the elation afterward. Even defeat had its bittersweetness, because we felt it together.

It also helped that I had a family tie to professional sports. My cousin—whom I called my aunt just because she was much older than me—married hockey-hall-of-fame legend Bernie Parent, one of the greatest goaltenders of all time and a back-to-back Stanley Cup winner. He's probably the reason my brother and all of my cousins played hockey.

I would play street hockey sometimes with my brother at home. I wasn't very good, but I still had fun. My mom got me into tennis because she thought it would be a good way to socialize. I enjoyed playing tennis and loved the thrill of it. Just like in the hockey arena, there was this vibe around all of the competitions—the excitement of seeing what's happening and who's going to come out on top. Even then, I knew I wanted to do something in the sports world, because I knew that nothing made me happier than when I was in the thick of a game.

"KATE DELANEY HAS BEEN SHOT AT"

My first professional step on the road to where I am today was my first job out of college. I went to school with the intention of becoming a journalist like NBC anchorwoman Jessica Savitch, one of the first women to anchor an evening network news broadcast. I remember her as pretty, smart, and always doing edgy breaking-news stories. I thought it was so cool what she did, so when I graduated from journalism school, I got a job working as an anchor for a station in El Paso.

It wasn't too long after I started that I was asked to cover the elections in Chihuahua, Mexico, which seemed like a pretty straightforward assignment at the time. But when we arrived, we immediately knew something was up. The atmosphere was electric. The two parties—the priistas and the panistas—were forcing people to stuff the ballot box, and as we began filming I heard a sound like firecrackers exploding. Suddenly my cameraman, Richard Cortez, was pushing me out of the way, throwing himself over me as the crackling noise continued. Most of the people in the crowd ended up with cuts and bruised but thank goodness I hit the ground fast enough not to be shot.

It turned out that party representatives had started firing their machine guns into the crowd. Back at the station, the anchors for the evening news were scrambling, reporting over and over again that

"Kate Delaney has been shot at." For a few minutes, no one knew if Richard and I were still alive or what was going on.

That night, Richard offered to stay on the couch in my hotel room because the political parties were now paying close attention to the journalists on the scene and making sure they didn't film anything they didn't want to be filmed. He was worried that I stood out and would be a target as an American journalist and he convinced me it wasn't safe to be by myself.

When we finally got back from that story, I remember asking myself if this was really what I wanted to do. Did I really want to be traipsing all over the place and winding up in situations where I was being shot at?

I still wanted to be a journalist, but the sports world seemed a lot safer, and that event helped to push me a little more in that direction.

BEING AUTHENTICALLY YOU

To be a great speaker, a great talk show host—to do anything where you're putting yourself out there on a regular basis, you have to be confident. There are always going to be detractors, but you have to stick with it and be confident about being yourself. Don't let people plant doubts in you, but don't go to an extreme in the other direction, either. That is, don't let your ego become so big that your confidence becomes arrogance. There's a middle road that successful entrepreneurs walk, where you believe in yourself but you don't think so much of yourself that you're not willing to listen to and learn from others—a place where you are comfortable with being your authentic self.

> *Don't let your ego become so big that your confidence becomes arrogance.*

When I moved away from Las Vegas, I found myself sitting on the airplane next to this nice older couple. I said hi to them and then, once the plane took off, I broke out my notebook and pen and jumped into the never-ending process of coming up with ideas for my show. The flight was a few hours, so I had time to really dig into what I could do that was unique and fun and would be engaging to my audience. I jotted down a bunch of thoughts, including one that I was so excited about that I wrote it in really big letters: dungeon.

I was so absorbed in the show idea that I almost didn't hear my seat neighbor when she said, "Excuse me."

I looked up, startled.

"I'm so sorry, can I ask you a question?" she said.

"Of course," I replied.

"What are you doing with a dungeon?" she asked.

I must have looked confused because she quickly gestured toward my open notebook.

"I didn't mean to look at your work, but I couldn't help seeing the big word 'dungeon,' and my husband and I are curious as to what it means."

I just started to laugh.

"Well, I'm a sports talk show host and I'm moving to Dallas to be on the radio network The Ticket, which is a big break for me," I said. "I'm going to be on the air this Monday, and I'm coming up with some things that I can do on the show besides the normal 'Here's what's happening with the Cowboys; what's wrong, what's right, and what's up with the players.'"

She was completely floored, and we ended up talking for the rest of the trip. They were so excited and impressed that they couldn't wait to tell everyone in their neighborhood to listen to me. One of the last things the husband said to me as we went our separate ways was "Don't worry. You're going to be fine because you're confident."

It was in that moment that I realized that confidence really is a game changer. You need to have that belief in yourself and your abilities—you need to be comfortable with being yourself, or people are going to sense that you aren't. If you doubt yourself, they'll know it, just like they'll know if you think too much of yourself. In either case, they'll stop listening to you. But when you're authentic with people, it shows—and it attracts people to you.

> *"Don't worry. You're going to be fine because you're confident." It was in that moment that I realized that confidence really is a game changer.*

The Dungeon idea ended up going over really well. It wasn't a whole bit like my Sports Jeopardy segment, or the mystery caller bit; instead, it was a signature thing. Keep in mind that it was the 1990s when I did this—a time when you could be a little sillier on the air—and I didn't use it all the time. The Dungeon was basically a sound effect of this heavy door squealing open, followed by a blood-curdling scream and then the sound of the door slamming shut. If someone in the sports arena did something brutal, like drugs or steroids or something really offensive, or if someone missed a really obvious question in the Sports Jeopardy game, I would throw them in the Dungeon.

On the other side of that, since I was a princess and all, I would also "knight" people. There would be the sound of a sword sliding from its sheath and a crowd cheering as I dubbed someone "Sir" whatever for saying something brilliant or answering a particularly hard trivia question.

Again, I didn't do either of those things often because I didn't want it to become obnoxious, but I pulled them out every once in a while. People loved them, and they quickly became part of my personal branding.

I probably would have gone forward with the Dungeon idea even if I hadn't had that conversation on the plane, but that couple reminded me of the value of being my authentic self and sticking with it, despite the circumstances that try to drive one into arrogance or self-doubt.

IT'S OKAY TO SAY "I DON'T KNOW"

People crave authenticity. They can sense it, especially in speaking. You can tell when you're in front of people and when you're on the radio—if you aren't being yourself, you don't sound as confident, which means you don't sound relaxed, which means you sound uncomfortable. I don't know about you, but I find it hard to listen to someone who sounds uncomfortable, much less learn from what they have to say.

In the beginning of my career, I was pretty much alone in my field as a female national radio sportscaster, so I felt like I had to really know my stuff—everything from the dawn of sports to the name of the center fielder who was replaced yesterday by whomever in the minor leagues. But there's so much history to sports and so much new history being made every day that it's impossible to know every-thing. When I tried to, it sounded forced—I wasn't being myself, I was just listing off stats or concentrating on the answer like it was a final exam. But once I was able to get out of my own head and realize that I couldn't know the answer to every question, I was able to find my personal confidence. I became okay with saying, "I don't know."

Most of us want to seem omniscient, like we know the answer to every question, especially in situations where we want to seem like we've got it all under control, as I did during that crazy trip on the Cowboys charter in chapter 2. But the fact is that you really should be asking questions. The more powerful the questions you ask, the better the results you're going to get and the better you can produce the outcome someone is looking for. The impression this gives is not that you don't know what you're doing, but rather that you care enough about the other person to find out exactly what they want.

> *I was able to get out of my own head and realize that I couldn't know the answer to every question, I was able to find my personal confidence. I became okay with saying, "I don't know."*

THE ONLY "SAFETY" IS ON THE FIELD

The sports world is a tough frontier for women. Just look at former professional softball player Jessica Mendoza, who in 2015 was the first woman to call a Major League Baseball playoff game on ESPN. Shortly after she joined hosts John Kruk and Dan Schulman on the air, out of nowhere, Atlanta radio show host Mike Bell started berating her on Twitter, writing things like "Really? A women's softball slugger as guest analyst on MLB Wildcard Game? Once again ESPN too frigging cute for their own good."

Jessica knew the game inside and out, but this guy wouldn't stop giving her flak. And for what? Apart from being a woman, what made her different than anyone else calling a game? Some announcers are former athletes, like John Kruk, who was a slugger for the Phillies, and others never played the game but are incredible play-by-play guys, like Dan Schulman. Jessica played, and she did a good job calling the game. You could criticize the woman if she didn't, but she was fine.

The entertainment business—and really most businesses—are shaky, subjective worlds. None of us know what's going to happen tomorrow, and as good as we may be at what we do, we're all vulnerable. The key is in knowing, without a doubt, that you love what you do, and that the path you're on is focused on that.

In the case of sports talk radio, I could get dropped by a new program director who comes in and just doesn't like my show or thinks that not enough of the affiliate stations like it. But that doesn't mean I pick up my bag and go become a lab technician or a mechanical engineer. It's a curveball, sure, but I've chosen my path and I'm sticking with it.

Take that job I was turned down for on the West Coast—the network where the general manager took my name off the list because he didn't like the idea of women on the radio, let alone doing sports. Funny enough, six years later I got an email from that same network. The original GM was gone and the new program director, Andrew Ashwood, wanted to know if I would be interested in doing a weekend show for them, which I could do from where I was in Dallas.

I never thought I'd hear from that network again, but if I'd given up on radio, like a lot of people were telling me to do at the time, that opportunity would never have come back around.

Of course, sticking with it comes with its challenges, too, and sometimes we have to be reminded how much we truly enjoy the path we've chosen by leaving it for a while.

DELAY OF GAME

Later on in my career, when I decided to become a professional speaker, I was excited, but I was also really overwhelmed. I didn't realize how much time management went into everything, from coming up with what I'm speaking about, to pitching, designing and updating my website, managing taxes and contracts, reserving dates … all of it. There was so much business to be done outside of my regular work with NBC, yet once again I wasn't asking questions or reaching out to people who could help me. I just tried to figure things out on my own, and after a while I became incredibly frustrated. I was making hardly anything, and people were asking me to speak for free all the time, so one day I just decided that I couldn't do it anymore.

There I was, the never-say-quit optimist, and I was quitting because my job was killing me. I put both radio and speaking aside and decided to go do something else, and that something else turned out to be selling custom homes.

The idea came from someone I met at the tennis club. "You could sell salt to a snail," she told me. "Have you ever thought about selling custom homes?"

I had never thought about it, but I decided to give it a shot. I applied, took a ridiculous personality test only to learn that I wasn't great at paperwork but fabulous at everything else, and soon found myself in a model home in this beautiful neighborhood, baking fresh cookies every day and talking to people about their granite options.

It did not take long for me to realize that yes, I have an engaging personality, and yes, I like people, but I did not—absolutely did not—like selling custom homes. I would stand in this house all day, and people from the development would come in complaining about how the oven light in their new Cherrystone house wasn't working or how the light switch was falling apart, and the only thing I could tell them was "Talk with the builder." Then other people would come in who were interested in buying a home and I'd have to show them the plans and walk them through finishing options, and all the time I'm thinking, "I hate this, I couldn't care less."

It took about two and a half months and a trip home to Philadelphia to realize that I couldn't do custom home sales. It wasn't where my heart was. I knew what I should be doing and I needed to get back into it.

It was a good awakening for me, and because of that little zag in my path, I was able to look at what I wanted to do with fresh eyes. I started talking with other people in the business, eventually working it out so that I could do radio and speaking without completely overwhelming myself.

It did not take long for me to realize that yes, I have an engaging personality, and yes, I like people, but I did not—absolutely did not—like selling custom homes.

Just because I like people and I can talk to them easily doesn't mean I would be good at any job that involved those skills, and the same goes for any other career. For instance, an attorney may be great at filing orders and staying on top of the court process, but they may fail miserably at actually going to trial.

A great example of this happened while I was working for the huge sports network WFAN in New York. The program director, Mark Chernoff, believed in me and hired me over several other hosts vying for the job. I had my show and also filled in when needed. On one of those days filling in, I remember talking about the Giants,

Jets, everything New York, when someone let me know that the guy filling in after me was a New Jersey Devils player.

Somehow his agent got him this radio spot, probably just to try him out and see how he did. I wrapped up my show just in time to see him pull up in a limousine and walk in with this little entourage of people. He shook my hand when I came out of the bullpen area and he was super nice, but he looked a little worried.

"We were listening to you in the limo," he said to me. "Boy, you're good."

I thanked him, and he added, "So you were talking about what's going on in football, right?"

I nodded, and he shook his head. "I don't really know all that," he said. "I gotta say, I'm kind of worried."

When his agent suggested the gig, he probably thought it would just be talking hockey, and that guy could have skated circles around me or just about any other sportscaster when it came to hockey. He knew all the nuances, a ton of the history—everything he needed. But in most sports talk shows, you have to talk about everything, and he'd only just realized that.

A couple minutes later, the producer called me in and asked me if I could stay with the hockey player for a while and help him get the hang of the show, which I did. I fielded sports questions until someone called up with something about hockey—usually a Devils fan—and then I let him answer it. In the meantime, I asked him all the questions I could about hockey and made him feel as comfortable as possible.

That was his first and last radio show. At some point, someone— maybe his agent—told him that he had a great voice, so why not talk sports on the radio? And he thought, "Why not?"—not realizing that there's so much more to it than just talking about one aspect of the sports world. There's all the behind-the-scenes work, too. The prep, the scheduling, thinking about what you can talk about that will interest people in Charlotte and Philly and Cleveland and Louisville, and everywhere else your show airs. You have to love all of the aspects of the job, not just one little part of it.

LEAP AND THE NET WILL FIND YOU

Doing what you love is not easy. It's not "secure," either, which scares a lot of people. But truthfully, as much as people talk about the concept, there is no such thing as job security. Not really, because you never know what could happen. The bottom could fall out of the market or the boss could pass away suddenly and the business is immediately liquidated. Security is an illusion.

Then there's the money factor. So many people chose a path or continue on it because of the money, but if that's all you're doing—chasing the money—then you'll never get there. You'll never have enough money to make you as happy as doing what you love. If you follow your passion, the money will come. Leap, and the net will find you.

The same goes for any business. When you're an entrepreneur, you're leaping all the time. How many times do you fail before you have success? And then, how many times do you fail again before you have another success? But you have to be willing to take those leaps or you'll never have those successes. Of course, there are always easier ways to do things and easier paths to take. I could have stayed an anchor at a local news station, for instance, but then I never would have experienced half of what I've experienced in life. I wouldn't be who I am today and I would not be happy.

It's also important to understand that getting to where you want to be in life is not a fast journey. As with anything—sports, radio, writing, business—you have to build it over time. You have to be prepared to stick with it and, just as importantly, you have to keep a positive attitude. The more time you spend thinking about the challenges and getting yourself down about the nitty-gritty aspects of the job, the harder it will be to turn the next corner and take the next step up.

Be willing to venture into the unknown. Don't just stick with a track because someone told you that you should become this or that. Take risks, walk off the path and find something that pushes all of your happy buttons. The road to doing what you love is never straight—I know mine zigzagged all over the place, so much so that I sometimes think of it as San Francisco's famously crooked Lombard Street. There were times I realized I wasn't headed in the right direction and had to reset, but the most important thing you can do is to keep trying. Leap, and the net will find you. Maybe not the first time or, like Edison and the lightbulb, the thousandth time, but it will, and then you'll realize that all that trying was worth it.

Take risks, walk off the path and find something that pushes all of your happy buttons.

PLAYMAKERS: RUTH HEDGES, ROBERT KRAFT

In 2012, Ruth Hedges knew there had to be a way for people who didn't have a ton of money to invest in a start-up company—a thought that led her to become one of the pioneers of crowdfunding. There was no road map for what she wanted to do, so she, along with a small group that made up the original Crowdfund Intermediary Regulatory Advocates (CFIRA), began drawing it.

It began with writing the crowdfunding bill that went into the Jumpstart Our Business Startups (JOBS) Act in April 2012, allowing accredited investors to invest in smaller firms. Then Title III of the act, which took more than two additional years to pass, allowed nonaccredited investors to do the same. It was a huge achievement, particularly since the sale of small stocks and bonds has been prohibited in the United States since the Great Depression. But today, thanks to Ruth and her team, a start-up company can raise up to $1 million from investors in amounts as small as $1 without having to get involved in any expensive registrations with the SEC.

This wouldn't be possible if Ruth hadn't stuck with her idea and her belief that this type of investing was viable. Ruth knew this would be a big win for everyone who wanted to invest but didn't have limitless capital.

After building a new software application for business plan writing, Ruth had been disheartened to learn that few people could use it. It was the height of the recession, and she was told that no one was writing business plans anymore because there was no funding.

"So I said, 'Wait a minute, I didn't work this hard to just roll over on this story,'" Ruth said when she sat down with me for an interview on ForbesBooks Radio. "'What do you mean there's no funding out there? Let's go solve this problem so I can get back to the business plan world.'"

The problem, it turned out, was far more widespread than she thought.

"I got together with a group of people who were frustrated with the problem of accessing capital because the banks, the VCs [venture capitalists], and the angels had completely stopped. There was no money moving anywhere," Ruth explained. "We joked that it was 'going to take an act of Congress' to get it moving again—and it did. We went to Congress with a bill we wrote called the Startup Exemption, and it took us seventeen months to get it passed, which was fast because it just made sense to everyone. The U.S. Chamber of Commerce got involved, Steve Case from AOL got involved, and on April 5, 2012, President Obama signed it into law."

"There are piles of business plans out there," Ruth added. "Innovators who graduated twenty years ago with some brilliant idea … the cure for cancer could be sitting in one of those tech transfer offices, for all we know. If crowdfunding had been around then, they wouldn't have had to wait for funding approval—they could have just gone to the crowd. Who wouldn't want to back one of these smart kids?"

Ruth wasn't afraid to knock down walls to make it possible for small companies to get much-needed funding, and she stuck with it until the bill passed and the SEC published the official rules around it almost four years later. She's a remarkable example of sticking with something until you're able to make it happen—which is an attitude and approach to life that legendary New England Patriots owner Robert Kraft is very familiar with.

Kraft was already a successful businessman when he began the long struggle to purchase the New England Patriots. Kraft had been a Patriots season ticket holder since 1971 and tried to purchase the team from owner Billy Sullivan in 1988, only to learn that Sullivan had sold the majority interest in both the team and Sullivan Stadium to Remington Products owner Victor Kiam. The stadium, however, fell into bankruptcy that same year and Kraft purchased it for $22 million.[1]

The stadium was outdated and considered practically worthless, but it came with a lease to the Patriots through 2001. Meanwhile, Kiam sold the team to businessman James Orthwein in 1992, who held onto it until 1994, when Kraft finally bought the team from him outright for $172 million.[2]

The year Kraft bought the Patriots was the first year they had a completely sold-out season, making it to the playoffs for the first time in eight years. Every season since then, from preseason to playoffs, has been sold out. In 2002, Kraft built Gillette Stadium for the Patriots, and today they're one of the most respected teams in the NFL.

Who knew that Kraft would go from being a fan in the early 1970s to owning Sullivan Stadium, then the Patriots, then building Gillette Stadium? After he took over, getting a ticket to a Patriots game is about as easy as eating soup with a fork, and good luck on getting season tickets—as of 2017, the wait list was averaging around

---

1   Robert MGC and Thomas Jr., "Sold! Time to Call Them the New England Permanents," The New York Times, last modified January 22, 1994, https://www. nytimes.com/1994/01/22/sports/sold-time-to-call-them-the-new-england-permanents.html.

2   Ibid.

fourteen years (though not as bad as the thirty-year average wait for Green Bay Packers season tickets).

When you're passionate about what you want to achieve, the biggest hurdle to doing it is endurance. From the very beginning of my career, people were always trying to discourage me—especially the ones who were well intentioned because they could see how hard it was for me. They would see me struggling and it would look like I was getting no traction, that I was just getting rejected, and they would encourage me to quit.

But I wouldn't. Instead, I would just keep reaching for that brass ring. (I actually never really understood that analogy until I was in Santa Cruz, California, and saw an old-fashioned carousel with a true brass ring stand. Every time the riders went by, they would lean off their horses and try to grab it so they could win an extra ride, but inevitably they'd miss. People would lean as hard as they could and just miss it over and over again, and it was rare that someone actually took the risk and leaned hard enough to grab it.)

If you're willing to take the chance, put the effort in, and stick with it, you can always grab the brass ring. Leap, and the net will find you.

CURVEBALLS

Do you feel stuck in your job? Do you live for the weekends and dread the weekdays?

If you answered yes to the questions above, here's something to think about: Visualize your life and what it looks like doing what you really love. See it and write it down every night before you go to bed.

What will it take to get you to take the leap? Take action every week, even if it's something small. Small leads to big, and little victories will help you move a step closer to doing what you want to do in life.

CHAPTER 4

TEAMWORK

*No one on the team is worried about the next level
and that's why we are where we are right now. It's
not just me, it's Michael, Cameron, and Damon.*

PGA TOUR PRO JORDAN SPIETH REFERRING
TO HIS CADDY, COACH, AND MANAGER

Games aren't won by one person, just as lofty goals can't be achieved by one person working completely alone. At some point, you need help. You need a team to support you and a mentor to guide you along the way, sharing the wisdom they earned for years before you came on the scene.

My pal and former NFL superstar, Russell Maryland, was drafted in 1991 out of Miami as the number one pick because of his incredible defensive skills, but he quickly realized that he wasn't the big man on campus anymore once he found himself in a locker room full of superstars. He struggled for a while with this new dynamic until a more seasoned teammate, Jim Jeffcoat, took him under his wing, helping him survive and ultimately thrive with the team. Once he got his feet under him, Russell went on to be a major player on three teams that went on to win Super Bowls.

For my part, teamwork appeared in many forms throughout my life. Even though sportscasting may seem like a one-man job, there's plenty that goes on behind the scenes, with multiple players, to make each show happen. And often some of my most valuable team members are not even aware of the important position they play.

My mom, for instance, was always my biggest advocate. Every time I hit a rough patch, she was there, encouraging me and reminding me that I'd never been the kind of person to swim with the current. She was there for me and my brother countless times, so when it came time for us to be there for her, neither of us hesitated.

It was Christmas of 2012, and my brother and both of our families were in Tampa, Florida, doing our best to make everything perfect for Mom, who was in the late stages of cancer. I remember that I was putting together dinner when I got a call from John McConnell, once considered to be one of the most powerful men in radio. He was running the ABC network at the time, which meant that when he called, I answered.

"Get your resume tape together now," he said.

"What?" I said, surprised.

It wasn't for ABC, he explained. It was for NBC. The network had been quietly putting together a sports radio network, but not too many people in the industry knew, and I was one of the first calls he made when he found out about it.

Mom could hear me on the phone sounding stressed. There was no way I was going to take time out of this Christmas to update my resume, let alone pay my producer in Minneapolis extra to help put it together, but she insisted that I do it. It was a huge opportunity and she didn't want me to miss it. So I worked on it. Mom died three weeks later.

The NBC gig wasn't a sealed deal just because McConnell told me about it. I still needed my advocates and teammates behind me to make it happen. Fortunately, one of those advocates, T.J. Lambert, had a connection at NBC and reached out to the network's program director, Jack Silver, to recommend me.

It was five or six months after I sent in my resume and tape, and long after T.J. put in that good word, that I got a call from Jack asking if I would fill in for the Memorial Day holiday. The audition was a one-time fill-in for Emmy-award-winning sportscaster Newy Scruggs, who also happened to live in Dallas, which worked out perfectly because I was able to use his studio. Jack liked my work enough that he asked me to start filling in here and there.

Eventually, a weekend gig opened up and Jack began bouncing the idea around with network management that I should get my own show during that slot. Not everyone was on board with the idea. There were plenty of other people out there vying for that spot— award-winning broadcasters, famous people, all kinds of options, but it just so happened that the network's newest senior vice president, Bruce Gilbert, used to work in Dallas as the program director of KTCK before he joined the Fox Sports Radio Network. We'd never worked together, but he'd heard me on the air and, in fact, had recommended me before to a network in Baltimore. So when they asked him what he thought about me doing a weekend show, he said, "Absolutely, I'm all for Kate! It would be great if we could get her." It was that recommendation that pushed me over the top.

If it hadn't been for those two, I never would have landed this amazing show on NBC. You can imagine that the big challenge in syndicated sports radio is in getting programming that the network affiliates like and choose to air. And talking sports in syndicated radio is a whole different ballgame than in local radio. When you're syndicated, you need to appeal to fans in Minnesota as much as you appeal to fans in Louisville and Miami. It's a giant net, but it was one that the team at NBC Sports Radio felt confident I could cast.

SPORTSCASTING

I knew I could appeal to NBC's numerous affiliate stations, but I also knew that I needed a solid team to back me up. If, say, we needed to tape something with a bigger guest or had to work around a tight schedule, a producer in California or even Jack himself would scramble. This not only meant working out a time to tape, but also coordinating between the Culver City crew—our home base—and me in Dallas to make it happen. And even though there were times when it didn't seem like everything would come together in time, our team always pulled it off.

I also had great resources when it came to creating the various benchmarks—what some think of as "bits"—that I use in my show. For example, during pro football season, I came up with a segment called "Nail the Score," which covers the Sunday night game on NBC. Sometimes I'll talk to one of the athletes connected to it, or I'll talk with one of the play-by-play guys, or I'll just have a beat reporter on for both teams. After we've talked it up for a bit, I Nail the Score.

"I think it's going to be 27 to 17," I'll say, or "I think Tom Brady is going to score three touchdowns," or whatever I think is going to happen. Then I go around to other people on the show, like the technical director or the update anchor, and ask them, "What do you think the final score is going to be?" People love it and it gets them talking.

Another benchmark I created was the Weekly Re-Rack, where we have a cool sounder (radio slang for a short audible cue, like NBC's three-note intro) and say, "Here is Kate Delaney's Re-Rack," followed by the top sound clip of the week, like the grand slam that pushed a team into first place, followed by four or five other highlights from that week.

Ideas like these were what allowed me to cast a net big enough to grab the attention of the NBC affiliate stations, providing me with this massive blank canvas that I could fill in with anything and everything happening in the world of sports. And my team was right there to help me, letting me know what stories were coming in and what sounded good, and even creating new sound bites, a big thing in radio since sound is so powerful.

> *Ideas like these were what allowed me to cast a net big enough to grab the attention of the NBC affiliate stations, providing me with this massive blank canvas that I could fill in with anything and everything happening in the world of sports.*

CROSS TALK

I always want my audience to feel like they're a part of Team Delaney—this fun inner circle where they feel like they're listening to a real person and not just some fake radio personality. To do this, I often engage in what we call a little "cross talk."

I'll give you an example. I come on from 3:00 p.m. to 6:00 p.m. eastern, right after a guy named Brian Webber. Right after the last segment of his show, Brian says, "Coming up next is my friend Kate Delaney. She always has a great show. Let's see what's going on with her," and then he and I will banter for five minutes or so about what's happening in sports or whatever we feel like.

It's fun because the talk is casual, off-the-cuff, and humanizing. We may talk about a big fight that just happened the night before, or we'll talk about something completely random and personal. For instance, one afternoon we somehow got on the topic of whether or not we used our real names for our shows, because sometimes people change their names in the business. I'm perfectly happy with my real name, but at one point in my career I had a program director who wanted me to change it. He thought my real name was too Irish sounding, he said, and suggested that I change it to Bailey Dupont. Way better, right?

So Brian would kid with me about that sometimes, or about something else funny, personal, or just something sports related, and in the process set me up like his teammate, passing me the ball (read: "the listening audience") and letting me run with it.

Brian wasn't the only fellow radio teammate that I threw the ball back and forth with over the years. Dave Smith was another show host who loved to cross-talk with me, and Chuck Cooperstein, the voice of the Dallas Mavericks, was always good for setting me up after his drive time show back in my Ticket days doing local radio in Dallas.

None of these guys had to help me out the way they did. They could have just signed off the air and gone to commercials, and then I'd do my thing. Instead, they supported me and treated me like a part of the team.

Chuck, in fact, actually ended up becoming one of my great advocates when we worked together at The Ticket in Dallas, where I arrived on the scene basically as an unknown. Supposedly people had embraced me on the syndicated show I'd been doing out of Las Vegas, but there I was, coming into a Dallas sports network and I wasn't even from Dallas. So to help me out, Chuck would listen to my show and give me advice afterward, and some of the best advice I ever received came from him.

"If you're going to criticize or praise or talk about the Cowboys or the Mavericks," he once told me, "you should go out and introduce yourself to some of these athletes and the people you're going to cover. That way they'll know you. They'll have seen your face and that you're on the radio."

So I did it. I went to the Cowboys practice field and introduced myself to Troy Aikman and the other players. Would I have done that if Chuck hadn't suggested it? Maybe not. But because he was a veteran talk guy and treated me like an equal, I respected his insights and learned a lot from him. He definitely helped me increase my odds for success by making that first trip to the locker room that I talked about in the beginning of the book.

THE MUSERS

A lot of the guys at The Ticket were supportive of me when I first started, and together we made a pretty good team. Apart from cross talk, another one of the ways they showed their support was by calling into my show and just chatting with me for a few minutes about this or that. The guys from the talk show *The Musers*—George Dunham and Craig Miller—were great about that, particularly George.

"Hey Kate," George would call in and say, "I'm washing the dishes and just heard you talking about the Mavericks situation," and we would go from there.

Another show host went out of his way to leave a note in my company mailbox shortly after I started at The Ticket. It looked like it had been written in crayon in the same doctor's scrawl that I use, but I got the gist of it: "We're so glad you're here. Welcome to the team."

I could tell that they were trying to build me up. I'm sure they would have done the same for any new member of the team, but it was encouraging to have them cross-talking with me, calling in, and generally letting their audiences know that "Hey, Kate's cool."

Even when our team got the news that the network was facing a big upheaval, I was glad to have them by my side. I was playing a big charity golf tournament with Chuck and Craig when we found out that The Ticket—which had been growing increasingly popular over the past year—was being sold. Chuck was the first to hear about it, and when he told us, the first words out of his mouth were "Oh man, we're in trouble."

When networks are sold, there's no telling if the new owners are going to keep you on, but thankfully it worked out for all three of us. Chuck went on to become the voice of the Dallas Mavericks, Craig stayed on The Ticket with his show *The Musers,* which is still airing.

KRLD, the huge sports network on the other side of town, was looking for a sports director, and with the purchase of The Ticket, my name came up as a potential candidate. Michael Spears, the program director at KRLD, ran my name by several people at the network, including Brad Sham, longtime voice of the Dallas Cowboys, and Eric Nadel, the respected and longtime voice of the Texas Rangers. Spears told me that both of them gave their enthusiastic blessing to bring me on as sports director.

That support from two well-respected guys in the industry was key in landing me a coveted spot in sports radio. There were probably a lot of people prickly about a woman taking the job of sports director, and both Brad and Eric could have suggested someone else for the role, but to this day I bet they don't know how much they had my back, and I scored another win in my sportscaster career goals.

NOT EVERY GAME IS A WIN

The great thing about radio is that you have these awesome moments and opportunities to nail it. Every day, you're working with a blank canvas and no net, and it's not like you're only having to come up with three minutes of clever copy before going to the weather person or back to the news—no, you're filling two or three hours of radio time with maybe an update guy and your benchmarks. It's either sink or swim every night, and when you kill it you feel awesome. But then the next night is another radio show, and the next day, another one.

There were detractors, of course, but I didn't pay attention to them. You can't. If you're going to be successful in any endeavor, you can't worry about the negativity. Instead, focus on your advocates—the ones who are buoying you and keeping your spirits up. These are your teammates and they're the only ones you need to pay attention to as you're going for the win.

> *You can't worry about the negativity. Instead, focus on your advocates.*

NAME YOUR DREAM, FIND YOUR MENTOR, BUILD YOUR ADVOCATES

Your teammates—those advocates who have your back when you need them—are so important at every stage of your entrepreneurial career. But just as important is finding a mentor, someone who has already taken the road you're starting on and can advise you on your journey. I have mentors now in the speaking world as I'm cracking that arena open more, getting onto bigger and bigger stages, but in the sports radio world it wasn't as easy. I had advocates, but in so many ways I was forging my own path. It was frustrating at times, and there were times that I wanted to just give up, but I knew that nothing made me as happy as I was when I was doing sports talk radio. I just had to leap and know that the net would find me.

The "net," by the way, wasn't just a financial one. Leap, and the money will come, but you also leap knowing that you have a network of advocates there to catch you. These are the people in your industry who can speak up for you, lend an ear, throw you a rope, and give you key insights when you need them the most.

As part of my work with ForbesBooks Radio, I did an interview with Libby Gill, author of the book *Hope Is a Strategy*. In explaining how she's thinking against the grain with the concept of hope as strategy, she pointed out that I'm one of those hopeful people that she writes about. And I am. I like to exceed expectations, and in that way I'm constantly in a mode of proving myself. I have to leap—put myself out there—and hope that I make the impact I'm intending to make. When I do, I find myself with a brand-new circle of advocates. They may be right there in front of me, shaking my hand after I come off the stage or reaching out to me while I'm on the air, or they're in the wings, recommending me to others but never interacting with me directly.

Building that team of advocates requires courage and yes, some hope. People will underestimate you and discourage you, and a lot of people give up on their dreams because they don't find enough advocates and lose that faith in themselves. You have to be comfortable with stepping out into the light, taking a chance, and leaping.

PART OF A MASTERMIND

As much as I am a people person, I was never much of a joiner—mainly because I don't like to give commitments and not have the time to follow through. But somehow I found myself involved in the

National Speakers Association and was eventually named president of the National Speakers Association in North Texas.

It began with a conversation over lunch. Association member Stu Schlackman invited me to speak and thought I should come to a meeting first as a guest, so I'd get a feel for the group. I accepted the offer, and instead of simply attending one meeting, I ended up joining the organization because I quickly discovered the power of having such a strong network of advocates and mentors to lean on.

When I was first starting out in the speaking world, I had no clue what to expect. And even though I found the association a little later on in my speaking career, they became my go-to resource for learning all the ins and outs of getting booked, finding my niche, and, most importantly, finding a mentor to guide me along the way.

The association was also where I discovered my first "mastermind" group.

The power of a mastermind group is unbelievable. Whether you need to bounce ideas around about the long-range plans for your business, how to get more business, where your business is lacking, what the trends are, or who the thought leaders are in your niche, a mastermind group will hold a conversation around your question, and together the members will narrow it down and find an answer.

My current mastermind group has made all the difference in the world for me. For instance, if I'm speaking about branding or about influential listening and I'm speaking to different industries, what better way to find out about the industry I'm going to speak to than to reach out to others in my group who are in that industry? If I just stayed in my own world relying on my own knowledge, I would never have the insights, or even know to ask the questions, that being in a mastermind group afforded me. It's the way you up your game in the field—the power of learning from other's mistakes, their know-how, their suggestions, is incredible. Whether you're just starting out in your industry or you've been in it for years, having that resource can leapfrog you ahead by years.

> It's the way you up your game in the field—the power of learning from other's mistakes, their know-how, their suggestions, is incredible.

There's a stat floating around that CEOs read sixty books a year, which I believe is completely true.[3] CEOs have this thirst for knowledge, for figuring out what they can do better, bigger, or badder than anyone else. They're always looking for a new nugget

---

3   Carrie M. King, "The Average CEO Reads 60 Books A Year – Find Out Why," *Blinkist Magazine*, last modified April 20, 2018, https://www.blinkist.com/magazine/posts/most-ceos-read-60-books-per-year.

of information that can have a powerful impact, so the smart ones go one step further and find a really good mentor or a mastermind group—which provides them with one more way to learn, in person and free to ask direct questions.

POWER ISN'T IN KNOWLEDGE— IT'S IN IMPLEMENTATION

Good mentors are not going to tell you "You must do it this way" or "This is the only road to success." Instead, they challenge you. And if you're not being challenged, then you need to find a different mentor or mastermind.

I made that mistake early on. My very first mastermind was made up of people I really liked, but it wasn't advancing me. We would come together every month and there would be a good sharing of ideas, but no one really challenged each other. Not only that, but we weren't holding each other accountable for what we said we were going to do, which is huge. As entrepreneurial speaker Colin Sprake once said, "Knowledge isn't power. Knowledge is potential power. Implementation is power."

That's so true. I could read all the books I wanted to, but if I didn't apply the knowledge I gathered, then there's no point. Failure to implement is failure across the board. And sometimes that's what separates someone with even one small success from someone who's not successful. If you work up the ideas for an entrepreneurial venture but never implement them, you're not going to get anywhere.

I enjoy implementing new ideas, which is one of the big reasons I'm in radio and speaking—every show and every speaking engagement is a blank page. Every audience is a new mix of people, so whether I'm speaking to an audience of two million that I can't see or of five hundred right in front of me, I have the opportunity to implement all kinds of new and innovative ideas to get people pumped up, listening, and engaged.

For instance, in my office, I have this big board listing out all of the current events, and it's my job to find ways to talk about them. On the radio—and with speaking, too—you're not just conveying information, you're painting a picture with your words. If the news comes down that some really talented college basketball player didn't get picked in the NBA drafts, I don't just say, "Man, that's a bummer." I paint a picture.

> I have the opportunity to implement all kinds of new and innovative ideas to get people pumped up, listening, and engaged.

"Imagine your entire life," I say. "You've spent every waking moment from the time you were five years old shooting baskets, getting up at four in the morning before school and coming home after school just shooting free throw after free throw for hours and hours, so that by the time you're nineteen years old you've shot over a million of them. It all comes down to this day and you're passed over."

There were also times in my career when I failed to implement my knowledge, and as a result I missed an opportunity.

One of these instances came after speaking with my good friend and mastermind buddy Christine Cashen about a speaking rejection I'd just received. I'd applied to speak at a pharmaceutical conference and was turned down, but instead of consoling me, Christine said, "Well, why didn't you get it? Have you called them? Did you find out what it was that would have made the difference?

"The more you know about why they chose someone else over you, the more you'll know how to present yourself the next time around," she reminded me. "It could have been no reason at all, or the person they chose could have had a background in the pharmaceutical business. You don't know unless you ask." She was right, if you want to increase your odds to win big, always find out why you lost out on a piece of business.

But I didn't even try to reach out for the information I needed to make a change in my speaking application approach after that rejection—a step that I knew I should have taken. It was a big reminder that I'd never get anywhere if I just took my licks and didn't bother to find out why—and then implement the changes needed to turn rejections into speaking engagements.

There are so many people in professional speaking, just like there are in the broadcasting world. You can't just stick with what you're doing and never learn from it, never grow. As Christine Cashen likes to say in her talks, "Be a rock star. Don't just be ordinary. Reach further. Reach beyond."

It's easy to do the minimum, to be mediocre. It takes going that extra step and not settling for "good enough." Reaching out to those who have gone before you for valuable insight and acting on that knowledge is what propels you from just another face in the crowd to the standout that you know you are.

PLAYMAKERS: ROGER STAUBACH, DAVE COOK, ANDRE AGASSI

To be innovative, to be forward thinking, you have to be open to possibilities and not just look at what you're doing. Even if you're killing it, are you still going to be killing it in the future?

This is where you need to have a strong team around you. Your mentors are there to provide insight into how they faced similar situations, and your mastermind group can drill down into any challenge you throw at them and help you think well beyond your own perspective. Your advocates support you and lend you a shoulder when you need one and lift you up. Together, your team is the net that catches you when you leap, and even if your road to success looks like a one-man operation, you're never going to make it without a team supporting you along the way.

In the introduction to Dave Gowel's *The Power in a Link,* former Cowboys Hall of Famed quarterback Roger Staubach wrote, "I've made several significant career changes in my life, including the transition from being a civilian to serving in the military; from the military to the NFL; and from the NFL to commercial real estate. Throughout these diverse careers, I've noticed a common trend relevant to any industry: exceptional relationships lead to exceptional success. ... To achieve more than mediocrity, one can hope to be surrounded by remarkable professionals who also perform beyond the call of duty. ... Such successful relationships require proactivity, a challenge that the best teams overcome together."

When I spoke with Roger "the Dodger," "Captain America" himself, about teams on the field from the perspective of someone who was both a star quarterback and the founder of an incredibly successful real estate company, he pointed out that "Collaboration is key, Kate, even to the point of selflessness. Having the right people around you means knowing that you're working with people who care as much about you as they do about themselves. That's the kind of team you want to be a part of."

Staubach exemplifies this quality in everything he does. Any of his teammates would say he was selfless, and so would those whose lives he's touched in real estate.

In considering who the members of your own team are, there are the obvious ones, like best friends, peers in the industry, and those mentor trailblazers who can guide you on what to expect, but there are always some less apparent parts of your crew who have just as much influence on your outcomes. These may be day care workers, your next-door neighbor, the one honest repair guy you know, or even your family doctor.

In the sports world, one of the most important members of a lot of major sports teams is one who gets very little recognition—the sports psychologist. And one of the most successful people in that field is Dave Cook. Dave has worked with several US Olympians, more than a hundred PGA tour pros, and multiple NBA teams—including the San Antonio Spurs, who won two championships working with Dave—and countless others.

My conversations with Dave are always fascinating, and each time we talk I walk away with something I can apply. One of his successes came with golfer Steve Lowery, who was having a hard time making cuts on the tour. Dave explained to Steve that what he needed to do was to call his own shots and create what he wanted to happen. Dave worked with Lowery the very week he won his first major tournament, and in 1994 he won a playoff by painting a mental picture of what he wanted to happen twenty minutes before the trophy presentation.

During one of our interviews, Dave explained to me that "We always have the opportunity to do something extraordinary when we embrace the pressure when everything is on the line and we feel the heat. Game day is every day in the corporate world."

Trainers, too, are among the unsung heroes of successful teams. Take Andre Agassi, for instance. Just one guy, but he's had enormous team support since childhood. In fact, there's a famous story that's often told about him playing a tennis match against football legend Jim Brown.

Andre was only nine years old when his dad bet Brown that Andre could beat him in a tennis match—and he did, three times. Later, when Andre was thirteen, his dad paid for him to go to Nick Bollettieri's tennis camp in Florida for three months, which was all he could afford. After watching him play for half an hour, Bollettieri himself called up Andre's dad and told him to take his money back— Andre had so much natural talent that he wanted him to play at the camp for free.

As talented as Andre was, however, his rivalry with Pete Sampras during the 1990s caused him to slip in the rankings, falling as far as 150th in the world for a time. In 1998, when Andre lost in the fourth round of the US Open, it was his strength and conditioning coach, Gil Reyes, who stepped in and got him to commit to building himself back up again. Gil got on him about his food and workout regimen, and even made him run sprints every day on a 320-yard incline that Gil nicknamed "Magic Mountain."

> "We always have the opportunity to do something extraordinary when we embrace the pressure when everything is on the line and we feel the heat. Game day is every day in the corporate world."

"Gil is the reason I've won more Slams after the age of twenty-nine than I did before," Andre told me during an interview while I was still in Vegas. "He's the reason I'm still playing this sport at an age when I can really appreciate it and understand it."

When it comes down to it, while some days you may see it as only yourself struggling against the world, you have to remember that there are other people out there rooting for you. We all need a cheering section, and the more we cheer each other on, the more we can celebrate each other's accomplishments. By helping each other and lifting each other up, just imagine how much more we can accomplish.

CURVEBALLS

Who's part of your net? Who are your teammates who are going to help you and pass on that valuable information, or recommendation, when you need it most?

Who are your advocates? The ones who swing for you, who are there for you when you're low, who help you get a foot in the door or give you a piece of helpful advice at just the right time?

Who are you cheering for?

CHAPTER 5

PERFECTING YOUR CORNERING TECHNIQUE: THE WORK AND HOME BALANCE

The biggest win I ever had was my son. I brought him up like a business in that I gave him the same value system that every great business has to have—charity, patriotism, responsibility, integrity, communication, God, and sticking with your principles.

PHIL ROMANO, FOUNDER OF FUDDRUCKERS, MACARONI GRILL, AND THE NETWORK BAR

I don't think I know a single entrepreneur who has a regular nine-to-five schedule. Even when you try to protect your time, it's really tough at points, so right off the bat I'm going to tell you that you will not always have an equal balance between work and home. If you're going to be in a relationship, your partner needs to embrace your ambition and understand that your world is never really going to be the world of nine to five.

When I first began chasing my career in broadcasting, I had to make that decision—career or relationship. I was married for a time back then, and while there are always two sides to a divorce, part of the problem was definitely that I was pursuing what I was pursuing. I worked weekends and late nights, sometimes staying out until two or three in the morning because it rained in the middle of a baseball game and we couldn't leave until it was over or they called a rain out.

But to entrepreneurs, that chaotic schedule is also appealing. You're reaching for that brass ring, and it's exciting. Great things happen, but there are also down times, and times when you're just digging in and waiting it out. Successful entrepreneurs realize that there are going to be failures, but if you keep going after the brass ring, eventually you're going to snag it. It doesn't matter if you're talking about a company worth millions of dollars or a start-up. Wherever you are with your business, as an entrepreneur you're always in it, drilling down.

Take Mark Zuckerberg and the dedication he and his team had toward launching Facebook. They were coding all day, eating pizza at three in the morning, sleeping for three hours, and getting back up again to track down and eliminate yet another bug, just to get the platform up and running. That kind of work ethic is almost impossible to balance with a relationship, so it does take some give on the part of the entrepreneur, but it also takes a lot of understanding from the other half of the relationship.

My husband, Paul, who is a professional photographer, is awesome. He embraces my wild schedule and I definitely make time for him, including him in what I have going on and making sure he's a part of it. Sometimes he even comes with me and takes pictures of my events, or just goes to games with me. I've even taught him some of the basics of producing so that he can help me on a set if he wants to.

That's how we negotiate our work-life balance. Of course, significant others don't have to be involved in your business, but they have to want to build you up and support that ambition. They have to be your cheering section, and you, theirs.

One of the reasons my relationship with Paul works so well is that, in his words, "I never know what's going to happen tomorrow, so every day is like Christmas."

That kind of perspective in a partner is what helps you get over even the darkest days in starting your own business. And just like a lot of people reading this book, I've not only come to the edge of giving up, I've actually stepped over the line to see if there really is more peace and security on the other side.

BREAKING POINT

A friend of mine named Annemarie, who worked for the government and managed to work her way pretty high up, found herself in a comfortable enough position to retire at the age of forty-seven. She was an incredibly hard worker, but one night, when I was staying in her guest room on my way to another speaking gig, she couldn't help but comment, "I could never do what you do. Now that I've been around you and seen some of the sets you've been on, I think it's cool and exciting what you do, but there are so many different people you're talking to and so many things you have to get to …" She shook her head. "I just couldn't do it."

What triggered that comment from her, I think, was the fact that I'd been up until three o'clock the night before, finishing a proposal that was due the next day. My first thought was "Yeah, that's part of being an entrepreneur." My speaking career is my biggest entrepreneurial pull, and while it's certainly not the only one, it requires the most time. Everything from meetings with speakers, bureaus, bookers, and other meeting planners, to crafting proposals, working with videographers, posting social media, jumping on phone calls, my weekly mastermind call, and a slew of other parts of the business added up to a large part of my daily grind. I have a wonderfully talented virtual assistant, but I'm still the ringmaster. In the midst of all that, if someone were to ask where I was building in time for myself, the only answer I could give them was "I'm not." And in doing that, I was unwittingly setting myself up for failure.

Being on my own, I know I didn't ask enough questions. I loved the work I was continuing to do with NBC and I loved the speaking world, which made sense to get into because of my career in broadcasting, but I didn't realize how much time management went into it all. I was doing everything, from coming up with what I was speaking about and pitching it to people, to coming up with exactly what I needed my website to look like so that it attracted the right clientele. There were so many questions: How are my taxes getting taken out? What am I asking for in my contracts? How am I reserving my dates? What does my pitch look like? Who are the people I'm pitching to?

Being on my own, I know I didn't ask enough questions.

I had all these questions, but I didn't ask anyone who could help me. Not that I didn't know people who could have—and happily would have—answered them, but by nature I'm a giver, not a taker, and asking questions was a kind of "taking" to me. I quickly learned that the speaking world wasn't as simple as getting on some stage, presenting some keynotes, and thanking everyone for the applause.

There was so much business to it, and I was quickly becoming frustrated.

What made it worse was all the people I would meet who'd say things like "Oh my gosh, you're so funny, I love talking with you and I'd love to hear you speak! You must be killing it." But I wasn't killing it. Not at all. I was hardly making anything, and people were asking me to speak for free all the time.

Despite my husband's constant support, I was having a hard time. It was overwhelming trying to control all that chaos and not knowing what to do because I wouldn't reach out to the right people. Sure, I reached out to a couple people who offered, but it turned out that most of them were just trying to take advantage of me and my lack of business acumen in the speaking world.

So one day, I—the forever optimist who never says "quit"— quit. It was killing me. I felt like I was going down a rabbit hole. I decided to just put it all aside and go sell houses for a while (for more on that story, check out chapter 3).

It took that break in my career to remind me how much I loved what I did—interviewing up-and-comers and entrepreneurs, and working in the worlds of business and sports interchangeably. It was a good awakening for me, not just on how much I loved my chosen career, but also on how much I needed to balance my time so that I could enjoy every minute of the world I'd chosen to live in.

BEFORE YOU BREAK, STRETCH OUT

Bloomberg Businessweek used to have a section in the back of the magazine called "How Did I Get Here?" that I read voraciously. I got so many leads for interviews from that section, but I also got incredible advice on business building. The article was usually the timeline of a well-known CEO, like Sara Blakely of Spanx, talking about where they were born, what their first job was, and how they eventually founded XYZ company, followed by their "lessons learned" at the bottom. One of those lessons that has always stuck with me was "Don't be afraid to ask questions; it shows how smart you are."

You can't go about building a business alone. Just as we talked about in the chapter on teamwork, you need to be able to reach out and build real relationships where the support keeps coming around full circle.

When I first spoke internationally, I would have made a terrible mistake on my contract if I hadn't told fellow speaker, and then-president of the National Speakers Association, Ruby Newell-Legner about the upcoming gig and my concerns over the paperwork. Without missing a beat, she asked me to send her a copy of the contract and replied within hours.

"Okay," she said, "here are the things you need to make sure you ask for. If you can't get them, it's a red flag. Don't take the gig."

She told me to remember I was travelling internationally and I should be paid in full by the time I was leaving for the trip. Also, to increase what I was asking for as a travel allowance as it was much less for the states. All contracts are different, but the standard is to receive half to secure the date and receive the rest no later than thirty days after you do the speech.

People are afraid to ask questions because they don't want to seem like they don't know what they're doing, but why struggle alone when there's a whole community out there that's willing to share the knowledge you need?

When you do ask that question, the next key step is listening to the answer to understand it—not in order to reply to it. This is a pitfall that a lot of people run into in the course of a conversation. You have a list of questions in your head and instead of focusing on what's being said, you're thinking about how you're going to ask those questions. However, if you're listening to that person and they say something you didn't expect, the smart thing to do is to stop them and ask them to tell you a little more about that. This is real interaction. It's not a fake question; it's a question that shows you're paying attention.

THE MILLION DOLLAR QUESTION

Of all the questions you ask in your working life, the one that should be at the top of your list is this: In the midst of balancing a demanding career with home life, how do you find time for your family and for yourself?

There are a lot of conversations these days around this question, and the answer is: it's hard to. It's hard to make yourself step away and take a walk, take a break, take a moment to look outside and see whether the sun is up or what season it is. This is another place where having that team around you is invaluable. My husband can be adamant with me about getting out when I'm getting too buried in my work. He'll make me stop and go play tennis or just take the dog for a walk, because he can see what's happening. He sees me grinding.

Like a lot of entrepreneurs, I get excited about completing something I'm doing. I want to get to the end of it, and I won't walk away from it until it's done and done well. That's one of the dangers of doing what you love, because it becomes so hard to walk away. You're always chasing and chasing and you don't let your foot off the gas, which can be good in helping you get things done that you're accountable for, but at the same time, if you don't ease up a little you're going to skid, or hit a wall and crash.

Chunking down the time like radio show segments is one approach that has worked for me. Instead of sitting for four hours straight, pounding copy or running through interviews, I'll take a break in the middle of it and go for a walk, or sit somewhere comfortable and just relax, even if it's just for twenty-five minutes. It's a necessary restorative pause that I likely would have never come up with on my own. I'm one of those people who has ten million things that I'm trying to get done and I'd burn out before I stopped. But I've learned that even when you're in the zone, you need to stop and take a mental break.

The key to making this work, however, is mind-set. Even if you decide to take a half day to regroup, or take a few days off for a vacation, if your mind-set is that you can never take a break, then you never really do. You're going to burn through those vacation hours answering emails, putting out fires, and generally making yourself more stressed out by the fact that you're not there, rather than enjoying the time that you have away.

Even when you're in the zone, you need to stop and take a mental break.

You really have to step back, find that balance, and set your boundaries. Be the person who can say, "Okay, here's a day." If you're on vacation, set your boundaries before you get there. Ideally, you should be able to step away entirely, but if you still need that check-in, limit it to a strict time frame and allow yourself the rest of the time to truly enjoy yourself. Let the work go. Cutting yourself off completely, if even for a few hours, is essential to keeping that balance.

I was guilty of this never-let-go mind-set when I first made the transition from employee to entrepreneur. I didn't set any kind of boundaries, and that quickly turned into a hamster wheel of trying to accomplish things at heart-attack speed while getting nowhere.

CALLING IN A (LUNCH) SUBSTITUTION

As enjoyable as lunch meetings can be, if you don't have a set time, you could be eating hours out of your day, not only during the lunch itself but on the drive time there and back. Taking one lunch meeting a week is fine, sure, but if you have five of those on your calendar in a row, it becomes a time suck. Instead, what I've started asking people who want to meet for lunch is whether they have time to join me on my morning walk instead. It's a comfortable thirty-minute circuit followed by a quick cup of coffee, and we're done at a set time. I make myself available, but during a time that I'm already doing what I intended to do, and in my own neighborhood so that I don't have to factor in drive time.

When you're an entrepreneur, it's so important to feel like you're moving the ball forward, but too many meetings, too many lunches, can get in the way of the time you need to get things done and feel good about them. Building a business takes a lot of work, but if you let that pendulum swing too far toward the relational side, it's tough swinging it back. You have to set those boundaries and create that balance.

DOING "THE SIX"

Around the same time I started time batching, I also got rid of check-lists. That is, I got rid of the huge, ongoing checklist that haunted every hour of my day and replaced it with The Six.

The Six, also called the Ivy Lee Method, is a productivity practice made popular by Charles Schwab in 1918. The story goes that Schwab asked well-known productivity consultant Ivy Lee to show him how he could get more things done, and Lee replied that he could do it—all he needed was fifteen minutes with each of Schwab's executives.

In those fifteen minutes, Lee explained exactly what they needed to do:

1. At the end of each day, write down the six most important things you need to accomplish tomorrow.

2. Organize that list so that the most important task is first.

3. The next day, concentrate on completing only that one task. Once it's done, move on to the next.

4. At the end of the day, put whatever tasks you didn't accomplish on tomorrow's list and repeat the process.

5. After a few months, Schwab saw amazing results with this method, and it's been a staple productivity process for entrepreneurs ever since.[4]

More recently, a friend of mine, Dawnna St. Louis, found a way to expand on the method. In her book, *6ix Kick-A$$ Strategies of the*

---

4   James Clear, "The Ivy Lee Method: The Daily Routine Experts Recommend for Peak Productivity," *Huffington Post*, last modified December 6, 2017, https://www.huffingtonpost.com/james-clear/the-ivy-lee-method-the-da_b_10257938.html.

Million-Dollar Entrepreneur, Dawnna describes how to identify your core strategy and then how to break your tasks for accomplishing that strategy into four quadrants:

CORE STRATEGY:

QUADRANT 1: INCOME

- Is it sufficient?

- Is it tracking with your future goals?

- Are you monetizing everything you can?

QUADRANT 2: OPERATIONS

- What is your process?

- Where are you on technology?

- How are you on people?

QUADRANT 3: FUTURE

- What are your goals?

- What's the mission?

- What is your vision of the future?

QUADRANT 4: THE CORE

- What is your expertise?

- What have I done that others would like to do?

- What do I know that others would benefit from knowing?

- What do I have that others would benefit from having?

- Using those answers from above: What challenge do I solve?

Now, every day when I get up, I have the diagram of my four quadrants right in front of me, and every day I know what I'm going to be doing, because I have the list I wrote out the night before of the six things I need to be working on. Then, every ten weeks, I check what's happening against my quadrants and choose to either keep doing an item, increase my efforts in an item, or get rid of an item because it's not working.

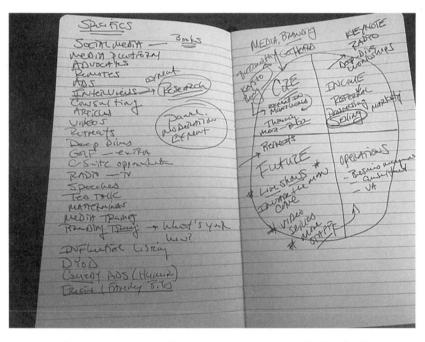

Say for instance that I'm writing an article for LinkedIn every week, but it's not working. I'm not increasing relationships and not many people are looking at it. This likely means that at my ten-week evaluation I'd probably get rid of that task and look at another way to increase my presence on LinkedIn.

For Dawnna, The Six got her out of a slump following the sale of her tech company. After weeks of waiting for the phone to ring, she realized that she had to take a hard look at what she was doing every day and whether or not her actions were helping her achieve her long-term goals.

As simple as it seems, The Six is extremely effective, because it helps you drill down on the most important things you need to accomplish. In the end, you're either producing income by moving the needle forward, building relationships that help your future business, or doing something innovative that's developing you professionally. Anything else is a waste. And in getting rid of that laundry list of "to-dos," you're also getting rid of the risk of overwhelming yourself, which is easy to fall into when you're, say, managing a speaking career, multiple radio shows, and heading up the National Speakers Association of Dallas.

In learning to almost subconsciously analyze the value of my actions and how I can apply what I'm doing on multiple levels, such as how pitching for a specific speaking event could provide me with new social media material and maybe even a blog post, I also finally began to look at how I spent my downtime. I do take time here and there for myself, but when I'm in the mood to do a little of both business and pleasure, I've found that there are some people right here in Dallas who are already two steps ahead of me.

BUSINESS AND PLEASURE: THE NETWORK BAR

Again, it's so important that we all take time for ourselves and just breathe, even if it's just in twenty-five-minute chunks throughout the day. Sometimes I'll cook or play golf or tennis with my husband. And even though I'm a voracious business book reader, every once in a while I'll pick up a "Pop Rocks" book—what I call those super easy stories that are just a pleasant burst of unreality. You get no nutritional value from them, but man are they fun to read.

But when I'm looking to strike a balance between business and pleasure, I'll either pick up a business book or go visit one of my favorite business concepts to date: the Network Bar.

Started by Phil Romano, the founder of Fuddruckers, the Network Bar is a membership club that welcomes entrepreneurs of all kinds, from investment bankers to media to tech. The concept is a combination meeting space and high-tech mecca—kind of like a brick-and-mortar LinkedIn.

"For any concept to be successful, it has to solve a problem," Phil told me during an interview. "People are networking, and they need tools to network. Right now, there are bunches of networking groups, but they're all fragmented— they don't communicate with each other. What we do is give them a place where they can go and meet each other, and we make sure the right people are there because the only way you can get in is with a membership. We made it look nice, with restoration hardware and comfortable seating, but really it's just a tool."

The idea is to balance the main two ways that people look at networking today. There's the traditional approach, with associations and conferences and monthly meetings, and then there's the tech approach, focused on connecting through apps and social media platforms. What gives the Network Bar that tech approach is its app, which lets you see who's at the bar before you even go. When members come in, the app shares some basic information about them to help people connect quickly, such as their name, title, where they work, and where they went to school.

Say I'm at the Bar, for instance. When I walk in, my profile illuminates on the app, letting other people know I'm there. If someone sees my name and the fact that I'm a speaker who focuses on things like innovation and influential listening, and they're wondering about how they can build their visibility and marketing, they might want to come over and strike up a conversation with me. The idea isn't to come in and start throwing business cards around, but rather to make meeting other people in the local business world easier. In addition, the Bar looks for members to serve as one of their monthly speakers and to serve as mentors for other members who are climbing the ranks.

Add to that the setup of the place—with a coffee bar, cocktail lounge, meeting spaces, and even some pool tables—and you have an ideal spot for business people throughout the Dallas area to share their business acumen with each other when they feel like hitting the networking scene.

For me, a place like the Network Bar is a great way to learn from the people in front of me, to mentor those coming up, and to stay plugged into the community—which is huge for all entrepreneurs, not just me, because again, that tendency to get buried in your work also leaves you cut off from the community that could be lending you a helping hand.

STAYING A PART OF THE VIBRATION

Community is something that a lot of us forget about, especially when we are so buried in our work. But when you shut out community, you shut out possibility.

How can you be an influential listener, or get people interested in you, when you're not out there being a part of the vibration of the business world? If you're so burrowed into your work that you're not getting out, not seeking conversation, not going to events, then you're not getting any feedback. It's just you, you, you.

It's easy for me to burrow in. I get tired. I'm on the road. I have a radio show or a speech to do. I have a business I'm putting together. I have excuse after excuse. But every time I've got something scheduled and I actually attend it, I learn so much. I'm a part of that circle, moving with the flow and vibing on the community and that constant input. By putting myself out there, I open myself up to the possibility of asking questions I might never have asked, or having questions asked of me that I never considered. Either way, I'm learning.

The smartest people are the ones who are always asking questions, and I can't think of better examples of this than the people I spoke to at a Mensa event.

I remember beforehand some speaker friends of mine being shocked when I told them that I would be speaking to Mensa.

"They'll be judging you," they said. "It'll be the worst group ever. Why do you want to do that?"

> *The smartest people are the ones who are always asking questions.*

But rather than being the worst group ever, they turned out to be the best, because all they wanted to do was learn. They were so active, raising their hands and asking all kinds of questions about the topic, which had to do with the importance of getting to know the vibe of the community you're working or presenting or selling in.

The topic was a home run, because there were so many aspects of the conversation that we were able to delve into, from the differences in colloquialisms from community to community to the way street signs are written in different cities. The feel is always going to vary and the key is that no one size fits all.

It was fascinating, and I got just as much from the Mensa members as they got from me. In fact, it became what I want all of my speaking engagement to become—a conversation, where it's not about me, it's about the audience. I want people to feel good and connected, like they got something real and valuable from our time together—either a nugget of information that they didn't have before or the beginning of an idea that just needed a little encouragement to get growing.

As you work to find balance between all the things you're juggling in life, always stay open to learning, even if it's just learning that you're not alone in the struggle. Give yourself some breathing room, and never let yourself get so buried in work that you miss out on everything that's going on around you. Reach out, learn, and become a part of the vibration.

We spoke about Christine Cashen briefly in the previous chapter. She handles an incredibly busy schedule that keeps her hopping around the country on a regular basis, but when she's home, she's all about her family. She drives her son to school, goes to her daughter's School of Rock practices, and has family dinners. And when she can, she plugs her family into her business, taking them with her to some of her more exotic speaking locations and opening her house up to cool speakers from all over the country, inviting them to stay with her family while they're in town so that her kids can meet them and feel more involved in her world.

Finding that balance, however, goes beyond the everyday. It also means knowing your limits when it comes to your career. As an entrepreneur, are you building a business that can one day run well—or better—without you? When you own your time, you know that it's ultimately you who's accountable for how that time is spent—and any entrepreneur worth their salt knows the value of every moment they're given. Spend it wisely.

PLAYMAKERS: TROY AIKMAN, USAIN BOLT, STEPHANIE LINNARTZ

For athletes, their sport is their business, and even when they know in their hearts that it's time to retire and take the next step, it's still a very hard thing to do. Look at former Dallas Cowboys quarterback Troy Aikman, who suffered multiple concussions in his career, one of which caused him to completely forget the 1994 NFC championship game against the 49ers.[5] Finally, after suffering two concussions within two months of each other,[6] as well as dealing with back pains that he needed to take epidural shots for before games,[7] the Cowboys forced "Iceman" Aikman to retire in 2000 at the age of thirty-four. Yet despite his injuries, Aikman didn't want to let his football career go and considered playing with a number of teams before ultimately

---

5   Matt Bonesteel, "Troy Aikman says he has no memory of playing in the 1994 NFC championship game," *Washington Post*, last updated February 3, 2017, https://www.washingtonpost.com/news/early-lead/wp/2017/02/03/troy-aikman-says-he-has-no-memory-of-playing-in-the-1994-nfc-championship-game/?utm_term=.3e904d292f70.

6   Will Brinson, "Report: NFL concussion research omitted Steve Young, Troy Aikman," CBS Sports, last updated March 24, 2016, https://www.cbssports.com/nfl/news/report-nfl-concussion-research-omitted-steve-young-troy-aikman/.

7   Tedd Archer, "Aikman offers cautionary tale for Romo," ESPN, last updated December 27, 2013, http://www.espn.com/blog/dallas/cowboys/post/_/id/4722370/troy-aikman-offers-cautionary-tale-for-romo.

accepting his retirement and moving on to a solid career in sports radio.

I've spoken to Troy a few times in my career. In fact, he was the first athlete I met in Dallas when I took sports talk host Chuck Cooperstein's advice and went to the Cowboys locker room. He is a consummate professional, and it's not a shock that he's done so well in the booth for Fox TV as a color analyst.

World-champion sprinter Usain Bolt, on the other hand, knew after more than a decade of competitive running that it was time to retire. At the age of thirty, the world's fastest man ran his final race in August 2017, followed by a farewell walk around London Stadium—the location of the second of his three 100-meter Olympic wins. "I was saying goodbye to the fans and I was saying goodbye to my events, also," he said. As for what he wanted to do next, Bolt pointed out that the first thing he was going to do was "Go out and have some fun—just to party. I need to go out and have a drink. I've had a stressful championship." After that, he's certain he's not coming back to competitive racing. "I think I've seen too many people return and come back into the sport and shame themselves," he said. "I won't be one of those persons."[8]

It's hard to accept the balance that retirement brings to your life when so much of your business is that excitement of playing and traveling and chasing a championship. The same goes for entrepreneurs—there's this innate sense of joy and accomplishment in facing down challenges that's so hard to walk away from. Even when one isn't considering retirement, stepping away from that all-out, all-in mind-set of living and breathing your business is exceptionally hard

---

8   "Now Retired, Bolt Excited About the Next Chapter," IAAF, last updated August 14, 2017, https://www.iaaf.org/news/feature/usain-bolt-world-champs-london-2017.

to do, yet it's so necessary to take that time and learn how to step away.

Stephanie Linnartz can speak well to that feeling of mentally sprinting through each day. As the global chief commercial officer for Marriott International, she oversees all of Marriott's revenue-generating functions and consumer interactions in relation to the organization's 6,500-plus properties and thirty brands across 126 countries. That's an enormous job that requires decision making on a scale that impacts thousands, if not tens of thousands, of people every day. Traveling, too, is a must, and Stephanie does it all with a smile on her face and still making time to step away and spend time with her family.

"I have school-aged children, a busy job that requires lots of traveling, and my husband works, too. We're the modern family trying to balance career and family, just like so many other families around the world," Stephanie told me during an interview with ForbesBooks Radio. "When people ask me about work/life balance, though, I have to say that I think that phrase 'work/life balance' is misleading. 'Balance' would imply equality, that you're spending equal time on both, and—at least in my case—I can't always do that. Sometimes work takes precedence, sometimes family. And it's tricky trying to figure out how to integrate both of them in a way that works for my job and family.

"I think it's about having priorities and acknowledging that you can't do everything. In my case, at this stage in my life, I focus on three things: my family, my health, and my career. I don't have time for anything else, because that's all of the hours."

One thing that's absolutely helped Stephanie—even though she admits that it has its good and bad sides—is technology. Not only has it allowed her to integrate family and work and health more, but it's helped with her global business, as well.

"Technology has some downsides, of course," Stephanie added. "But I look at it as a major net positive in terms of being able to balance and integrate my life."

As Stephanie, Troy, and Usain learned, you have to strike that balance. Every day—and on a greater scale, over the course of your career—you need to set those boundaries and stick to those clear limits between work, family, and self.

CURVEBALLS

What methods do you use to give yourself mental breaks throughout the day?

How do you balance time between work, family, and yourself?

How many times a day do you unplug from technology?

How many vacations do you take a year?

CHAPTER 6

WHAT ARE YOUR STATS? WHO YOU ARE AND HOW YOU SAY IT MATTERS

It is never too late to be who you might have been.

GEORGE ELIOT

"**W**hat do you do?"

This is a question that most people don't answer very well. I know I didn't for the longest time. It's a hard one to answer, especially when you're someone like me who has a lot of spinning plates. Am I a talk show host? A consultant? An author? An international speaker? And when you do pick one, the answer usually doesn't say that much about you.

When I began putting myself out there on social media, I quickly realized that my personal branding was about as thrilling as watching a cricket game when you're not entirely sure how it's played. First impressions are a one-time thing, and when your reply to "What do you do?" is as forgettable as "I'm an entrepreneur," then you're failing at one of your most important jobs—getting people to remember who you are and what you do, so that when they need what you do (or know someone who does) you're the first person who comes to mind.

Coming up with that awesome opening line isn't something that comes easily. It starts with having a basic understanding of what you do ("I'm an entrepreneur." "I'm a consultant.") and then narrowing it down to why you are who you are and do what you do. That "why" gives you an idea of the direction you want to go, even if you're not quite attached to the path.

My friend Jessica is a great example of this. A truly gifted architect, Jess is smart and beautiful with all kinds of degrees, but she was constantly losing out on jobs. She'd be outbid on one or she'd meet with the potential clients and they wouldn't go with her because she wasn't a very good networker. When she eventually brought the problem up with me, the first thing I asked her was "When people ask you what you do, what do you say?"

"I'm an architect," she said.

I thought about that for a minute, then said—because I know her and I know her portfolio—"Why don't you tell them this instead: 'Well, if you look at the skyline of downtown Philadelphia, chances are you're looking at a few of the buildings I designed.'"

She agreed to try it out, and a few days later I got a call from her.

"What a difference!" She said. "When I told people about the skyline, their first reaction was 'You're kidding, which ones?' And when I told them, they'd either been to it or knew what I was talking about, and would say something about how beautiful it was."

It didn't take her much longer to say than "I'm an architect," but just that little bit of depth made her so much more exciting and vibrant. An architect can design all kinds of things, from airports to public bathrooms, but when you're more specific and narrow down what it is that you specifically do, and present it in an engaging way where the person you're talking to can visualize it, then you've got a home run.

WHAT IS YOUR "WOW"?

I've done a similar exercise with audiences, where I dive into the crowd and ask someone to introduce me to the person sitting next to them.

"This is Tom," they might reply. "He's a great guy. Residential real estate agent with two kids. He grew up in Andover."

"No, no, no," I say, then I turn to Tom. "Tom, how many dreams have you made come true for families because you sold them a home?"

"Well gosh," Tom says, "Hundreds."

"Can you be more specific?" I reply.

And that gets him to start thinking about it, so by the time we're done with that short exercise, he's not Tom, the residential real estate agent. He's Tom, the man who has made seven hundred people's dreams come true because he found the right home for them.

If someone said that to me while I was trying to find a real estate agent, then there would be a good chance I'd ask for an introduction to Tom, or I'd certainly consider using him as my agent if that was how he introduced himself to me.

A good opening line isn't just about how you come across to others in person—it's also about how other people speak about you when you're not around. If you give someone a line about you that they'll remember, chances are they'll bring it up again when your area of expertise comes up in conversation.

This has come into play for me several times over the years, and on more than one occasion, it's given me the opportunity to spread the "What is your wow?" approach to others. One time in particular, a friend of mine called me up to see if I would be available for a speaking gig after one of the speakers dropped out unexpectedly. It was too late to fly me in, she said, "But could you do a keynote speech over Skype?"

"Sure," I said, though I'd never actually done one before. Fortunately, it turned out even better than I expected. I gave my talk, then did the audience interaction portion using someone in the conference room as my remote stand-in. With microphone in hand, she walked up to various audience members and held it up to them as I did the "introduce me to the person sitting next to you" exercise. Since this was an all-hands meeting for a manufacturing company, we met several people from all parts of the company, from call center employees to scientists.

Then we met Sarah. She was probably in her early twenties and sitting in the back of the room, doing her best to avoid being spotted, which only meant I was able to pick her out of the crowd more easily. I asked my assistant to hold up the microphone, and instead of asking Sarah what the person next to her did, I said, "So what do you do for the company?"

"I'm a chemist," she replied.

"Ah," I said. "Well, that must have taken a lot of schooling. So what do you do for fun?"

She smiled. "I'm a Frisbee champion," she said.

The whole room gasped along with me. Who would have thought that this quiet young chemist not only knew how to throw a Frisbee but did it competitively? Then she put the icing on the cake:

"And I've won an international competition," she added.

"How many competitions have you been to?" I asked.

"Oh, more than a hundred since high school, certainly," she said.

The room was stunned. None of them knew this about her. They just thought she was a chemist in sector 7-G of the company, or whatever part of the building she worked in.

"Then that's the way to introduce yourself," I said. "You're the Frisbee-throwing chemist."

You could tell from her expression how incredibly excited she was by this idea, and even though I wasn't able to follow up with that group, I'm sure she went on to use that introduction every chance she got.

A similar situation occurred at a conference that included a large number of attorneys. This time I was there in person, and I picked one person out of the crowd to tell me what he did for a living.

"I'm an attorney. I've been one for twenty-five years," he said.

"Okay," I replied. "In what kind of law?"

"Securities," he replied. So we took a look at what he did during his downtime, and it turned out that he was not only an excellent golfer, but that over the course of his game experience, he'd gotten no less than six holes in one. And it turned out that he'd hit them in different parts of the country, so we took the exercise a step further.

"Were they country clubs or resorts?" I asked.

He recalled that one was at a fancy club in the Midwest and another was while he was on vacation in the South. As he listed them all off, we discovered that he'd not only hit six holes in one, but he'd hit at least one hole in one in each quadrant of the United States. Just like our Frisbee-throwing chemist, that became the unique spin on his answer to "What do you do?"

WE'RE ALL SELLING IN SOME WAY

When you get down to the meat and bones of it, all of us are selling in some way. When you ask your spouse, "Would you like to go out for dinner?" You're selling your partner on where you want to go. When someone asks you what you do, you're selling yourself. You're selling your uniqueness—not in an awkward way, but in a way that's comfortable and reflects the real you, such as being a Frisbee champion or a really good golfer. And in being unique, you stand out.

That attorney has probably been introduced to thousands of people over the course of his career, but how many do you think remembered him? I'll bet you dollars to donuts it's not as many people as will remember him when he kicks off his "What do you do?" reply with "I'm a securities attorney who's hit a hole in one in every quadrant of the United States."

When you have it right, your "wow" isn't a pitch or an elevator speech, it's something that comfortably and uniquely reflects your why—and your why is the reason people buy, whether they're buying something from you or they simply want to have a closer relationship with you.

HOW YOU SAY IT MATTERS

After the introduction, there's the conversation. Simple enough, right? Once you're off to a good start with your "wow" reply, it should be easy to slip into a chat about your "why," but when you're talking in front of larger groups or, say, traveling to another country—or even another part of your own country—what you say, and how you say it, matters quite a lot.

This was made quite clear to me long before I got into the speaking circuit. In fact, it happened pretty early on in my radio career when I made that first big move from Las Vegas to Texas. It concerned vague directions and the words "FM 286."

Now, having lived in Philly for most of my life and only living for a brief while in Vegas, I was more familiar with Allegheny

County's color-coded belt system than I was with highways on the open plain, so when someone told me to look for "FM 286" I immediately assumed that I had to tune to a radio station to find out where I needed to go.

Remember, this is back when there was no GPS or smartphones, and cell phones were pretty rare. All I had was a gigantic paper map that I couldn't fold correctly to save my life, and these directions … and I was completely lost.

Finally, after going around in circles for far too long, I stopped at a convenience store to ask for directions. This part, by the way, just underlines the importance of that other life lesson I spoke about earlier—not being afraid to ask questions.

I walked up to the guy behind the counter and said, "Hi, I just moved here and I'm trying to find this house. Someone told me FM 286, but I've been flipping around on the radio trying to find it and I'm not getting anything. Is there something I'm missing here?"

The guy laughed hysterically for about half a minute before he answered me.

"Where are you from, gal?" he said in this thick Texan accent.

"I'm from Philadelphia," I said.

He laughed again.

"It means farm to market, sweetheart," he said. "You'll see signs around that say that, and that's what it means if someone tells you FM. You'll see them all over."

It wasn't unusual, he explained, to see FM signs in some city areas and right outside of the city, which meant that FM was typically a part of any given set of directions. What he didn't explain, however, was why the "FM" part of the road name was so buried in the directional signs, but I got the gist and thanked him for his help. I'm pretty sure I heard him laughing again as I walked out.

It was certainly an educational moment for me, and one that stuck with me the more I traveled. If the name of roads were the same on the sign as the name they're known by, it would make traveling by verbal direction so much easier. But I'll bet you can think of a road right now that technically goes by one name but is known locally by another. Once I became comfortable with travel around Dallas, for instance, I learned that the road everyone referred to as "Central" was actually called "75."

The issue is that people become comfortable with nicknames, especially when those around them know exactly what they're talking about. But what about when someone from Philly tries to find a farm-to-market road on the radio? That unintentional miscommunication can leave people driving in circles or just giving up on the trip altogether.

That exact same thing happens in business every day. People become comfortable with in-office phrases, acronyms, and shortcuts, never really thinking about them because everyone in the office knows the system. But what about when someone from outside the company needs to do business with you? Or when your company needs to interact with a similar company in another country—or even another state? If we can get culture shock just by traveling from one state to another, think about how complicated communication can become on a global level.

SLAYING THE SILOS

Businesses are typically siloed situations. They have their own culture, lingo, systems, and processes—all of which are so natural that when someone from that business goes to interact with another business, even one that's within the same parent company but in another country, they may get lost quickly.

If I'm speaking to Stanley Oil and Gas, for example, the way they speak about their business in Saudi Arabia is going to be different from how they speak to their branch in London or Houston. It's still going to be related to the main core of the business of oil, but how you handle crews and communication and outreach is going to be different in each locale.

When companies have more than one location, or when representatives from a company travel to other states and countries for business, one of the most important things they can do is learn to "slay the silos." And to do this, you have to be unafraid to disrupt.

What do I mean by disrupt? I mean coming back to that core life lesson again—asking questions. You have to be completely willing to ask questions when you don't understand something. That may seem elementary, but let me give you a quick example.

You have to be completely willing to ask questions when you don't understand something.

Think about the last time you were having a conversation with a client or even just a friend or relative. They're telling you a story about some-such-or-the-other, and in the middle of it they say, "… and then Rob goes into his whole thing on mind-body dualism. You know, that whole Descartes spiel …" and you nod sagely or say, "Oh yeah, good ol' Descartes …"

Did you really understand what that person was saying, or did you just agree because you didn't want it to seem like you didn't know what they were talking about?

You can likely trace this habit back to the schoolroom when the teacher told you to raise your hand if you had a question. The teacher would look around, you would look around, and since no one else raised their hand, you didn't, either. Why? Because most of us are afraid to be first.

You can't be afraid to slay the silo. You can't be afraid to disrupt. And the more you're an open book, asking questions and sharing answers, the more quickly you'll rise through the ranks—because whatever you give to the world will come back to you tenfold.

DO YOU HAVE A CULTURAL GUIDEBOOK?

Can you imagine if every business out there had a cultural guidebook? Not just for others, explaining the cultural terms and acronyms and shortcuts used by the company, but also for its own employees to refer to every time they communicated with companies in other locations. Remember the challenge I faced in trying to figure out "FM" in Texas? Your employees might be facing similar cultural challenges even if the conversations are happening within the same company in the same country. And when you or your employees venture outside the country, that's where you could really use a cultural guidebook.

I certainly could have used one the first time I spoke in Spain. The conference took place in the city of Toledo in Castile–La Mancha, central Spain. It's a beautiful, ancient city, but I wasn't thinking so much about sightseeing as I was about what I needed to do once I got there. In typical Kate/American fashion, I hopped off the plane ready to roll—check mics, check setup, go over itineraries, whatever needed to be done. But that was not how things were done in Toledo.

In Toledo, the mind-set is centered more on thoughtfulness and slowing down time. As much as the world seems to move at the speed of light, the people of Toledo liked to have a foot in both worlds— the old and the new. There I was, arriving in a tornado of "Hurry up and get it done," and the people of Toledo almost had to hold up their hands to stop me. "No, no, señora," one of the company representatives told me. "We're having a reception before you speak. There is no rush."

I was not prepared for that. A reception before the keynote? I was used to having receptions afterward, not before. And I was speaking midmorning, so it seemed to make sense to speak first and then eat and talk afterward. But instead, we talked and mingled and enjoyed some food before the talk—which was lovely in and of itself, because the company, in recognition of my being an American, made sure there was plenty of Coca-Cola and patties fritas (french fries) as part of the spread.

What was even more of a curveball for me was that there was no "hard" start time. We simply talked and ate, and at some point everyone began to walk to their seats and the MC for the event welcomed me to the stage.

And you know what? Even though I was thrown for a loop with the unusual schedule, I felt I did a better job with the speech because I was able to relate with the audience. I'd spoken to so many of them before I got on stage that once I was up there, I was able to include a lot of them in the talk, which just created a much warmer sense of camaraderie and depth.

Ever since Spain, I've tried to work that aspect into my talks—talking with the attendees beforehand so I can speak to them directly during my presentation. I didn't know others did the same thing until a friend of mine, a fellow speaker, told me that she called it "compassing the room." Even if there's not a reception, she said, it helps to get there early and talk to the attendees and get to know them a little bit. Not only do those audience members feel more engaged, but being able to speak to specific people in the audience makes it far more relatable.

The lesson I learned in Spain—apart from the need for creating a cultural guidebook for myself—was to slow it down. I didn't always need to be in a hurry. Even though we live in a hurried world, our business dealings, and even our relationships, can be that much better, deeper, and richer if we take the time to slow down and get to know where we are as opposed to where we're rushing off to be.

LEAVE ROOM FOR EDITS

Apart from learning to slow down, Spain also taught me the importance of learning to "leave room for edits." In other words, as often as I can, I leave time in my schedule for the unexpected. If possible, I like to arrive at the place I'm speaking a day beforehand because it not only takes the pressure off the hosts, cutting down on the chances that I'll run into travel delays, but it also gives me a chance to catch up with the event planner, meet with some of the company representatives, and compass the room before getting on the stage.

Leaving room for edits means acknowledging that you can't control everything that happens. Sometimes life happens and there's nothing you can do about it.

I had an opportunity to see this very statement in action in Phoenix during the National Speakers Association's annual convention, Influence 2016. I'd been asked to do this big panel on curating relevant and valuable content and was going to be conversing with reps from TEGNA Media, CBS, Google, and a host of other heavy hitters. It was a main stage morning event, right after the keynote speaker, and at least 1,500 people were expected to attend. It was a big deal, and an even bigger deal to me that I was asked to be a part of it.

I couldn't wait to get there, and—just to leave room for edits—I booked a flight that arrived a couple days in advance of the panel presentation so that I'd have time to run through the usual speaker checklist and pre-interview the other panelists.

Now, normally I fly American Airlines, but because the event was in Phoenix, I decided to take Southwest, since it had a better flight. But then, a few days before my flight, an unexpected router failure caused Southwest to ground its flights—an incident that resulted in more than two thousand flight cancellations, although at the time all I knew was that it had happened before my flight was scheduled, so it wouldn't affect me … or so I thought. Usually these things get straightened out quickly, I thought. The airline has people to get in the air and a reputation to maintain. The next morning, Southwest's CEO Gary Kelly was assuring people that the problem was solved and they were getting everything sorted out.

But the aftermath of that router failure was far worse than anyone imagined. I'd scheduled an early flight, and since this was one of those rare trips that my husband was able to take with me, he drove us both to the airport. On the way there, however, I got a call telling me that the flight was rescheduled. However, the representative assured me that I would be able to get on a flight the next day, which was scheduled to leave slightly before the crack of dawn.

Since I'd scheduled to get to the conference a couple days early, I wasn't too worried about it. A day delay just meant that I'd get there one day before instead of two, and I'd still have time to run through the checklist and speak with everyone, although it would be a little tight. So we went home and did the same thing the next day, leaving well before dawn to get to the airport.

And, once again, the flight was canceled.

What could we do? The panel was scheduled for the next day, and every other airline was booked solid between Dallas and Phoenix.

And even if I did get a flight with Southwest for early the next day, I didn't want to risk another cancellation.

As we sat there looking at the long list of canceled flights, my husband suddenly looked over at me and said, "We've got to get you to Phoenix. Get in the car."

"What?" I said.

"We're driving," he replied.

Every time I tell this story, the first answer I get is "You're kidding." But we had to do it. There was no other way to get there. Our bags were packed, so we just turned around, threw some water bottles in the car, and started the seventeen-hour drive to Phoenix.

We had to eat on the trip, of course, so we stopped at a couple of places on the way—this great little hole-in-the-wall restaurant in Las Cruces where they had excellent red and green chili. Other stops were brief to fill up and grab crummy gas station snacks. The rest of the time, Paul was on the phone, calling speakers to rearrange times and talking with coordinators to let them know I was on my way and figuring out what needed to be rescheduled to make it all happen. And while he was doing that, I drove—all 1,064 miles.

We finally pulled up at the hotel at 10:00 p.m. the night before the panel. We were both completely whipped and were helping the bellhops load our luggage onto a hotel trolley when one of them glanced in our car and said, wide-eyed, "Where did you say you came from again?"

"Dallas," I replied.

"Really?"

"Yup," I said. "Straight through."

"With a stick?" he said, looking once again at the center console. I smiled, "That I did."

The kid just shook his head and said, "You're a badass."

He didn't know who the hell I was or what I was doing there, but the fact that I drove a stick shift from Dallas to Phoenix made me a rock star in his eyes. It really hit home at that moment just how crazy it was to drive, but it was the only solution. Neither of us thought twice about driving a stick shift for seventeen hours; I had to be there.

> *The fact that I drove a stick shift from Dallas to Phoenix made me a rock star in his eyes.*

That trip was the perfect embodiment of how important it is to leave room for edits. When things don't go as planned, can you roll with it? Because if you can't, it makes things harder not only for you, but also for everyone around you.

PLAYMAKER: RUBY NEWELL-LEGNER

Ruby Newell-Legner, the founder of 7 Star Service, is a rock star in the customer experience world. Originally a swim coach, she developed an allergic reaction to chlorine and suddenly had to find a new focus, which she did when she attended her first National Speakers Association meeting in Denver. She quickly found that her coaching skills translated brilliantly into the customer service arena, and today she's known as the "fan experience evangelist." Ruby has spoken to more than 2,000 sports and entertainment organizations in nine countries—including NFL, NHL, and NBA venues, which is how I met her.

Yet even with her depth of experience in understanding the customer, cultural differences in varying countries can still sneak up on her.

Sometime in the mid-2010s, Ruby's company, 7 Star Service, was helping to open a huge water park that's part of The Burj hotel in Dubai. She was familiar with many of the customs in the United Arab Emirates, but one she wasn't aware of was that women aren't supposed to speak to men in the elevator.

Ruby is one of those warm, friendly super includers that can strike up a conversation with anyone. When she hopped on the elevator at her hotel, she didn't think twice about talking to the man next to her, who was dressed in a traditional thobe dishdasha. She just launched into this big speech, not even realizing that the man was stone faced and looking straight ahead, doing his best not to acknowledge her.

Someone on the elevator eventually made a hand signal to her to stop, and she did. And even though she unintentionally irritated that gentleman, she learned a valuable lesson about relations and customs in the UAE.

But that wasn't the last cultural faux pas for her that day. Again, Ruby is incredibly culture- and customer-savvy, but this was her first visit to the UAE, and though she'd done her homework there were some key points that weren't mentioned in her research. In this case, the fact that even though most Arabs, and certainly every employee at the water park, spoke perfect English, very few of them could read it. Based on the conversations she'd had with the company, she'd just assumed the team could read English as well as they spoke it, so every last piece of her training material was in English. One all-nighter later and a change to all the copy and it was fixed. She increased her odds to win big by killing herself to make the change, but how could she leave it the way it was?

I had my own, somewhat less stressful, culture clash in 2015 when I played in an LPGA Pro-Am in Irving, Texas, with a pro named Ha Na Jang from Korea. She was incredibly kind and just crushed the ball when she played. In fact, it turned out that she was a five-time winner on the KLPGA Tour and was selected as the KLPGA Tour Player of the Year in 2013.

When we met, she bowed and presented her business card to me with both hands, as was the proper etiquette in her country. I wasn't entirely sure what to do in response, so I took the card and thanked her. Later on, I realized that I should do the same back, so I presented my card to her in the same manner once we reached the back nine.

Doing your homework before you travel—whether it's to another country or another state—is critical. Whether you're speaking with or simply visiting another company, or even going to another branch of your own company in another location, make sure you and those traveling with you are aware of the customs and lingo of the area. Even simple things such as the names for streets and what people really call them can make a big difference.

Because of the challenges these cultural differences can create, a lot of meeting planners are starting to create "Know Before You Go" sheets, which is great for large company travel, but I would urge companies to do this for individual employees and visitors alike. Providing visitors to your company with a "cheat sheet" on culture can break down roadblocks before you even run into them, and making sure your employees are more capable of "speaking the lingo" when they travel can cut down on expensive mistakes (such as paying a cab to travel from point A to point B when a local trolley would have been ten times cheaper) and help them feel more comfortable during the journey.

Unexpected things happen—they always do. That's why being flexible is key and why these two life lessons should stick with you like glue as you go through life, both professionally and personally: leave room for edits and never be afraid to ask questions.

CURVEBALLS

What happens when the path you own changes? Are you adaptable?

Write down those times when flexibility served you well. What happened when a monkey wrench was thrown into your plans? Remember how you handled that situation, and think about what you would do the same and what you might do differently the next time you hit a pothole.

CHAPTER 7

THE ART OF INFLUENTIAL LISTENING

When people talk, listen completely.
Most people never listen.

ERNEST HEMINGWAY

C an you listen? I mean, really listen—it's tougher than most people think. In an era where the average human attention span is shorter than that of a goldfish,[9] real listening has become a critical skill.

Eight seconds is all you have before most people become distracted. That's eight seconds to pitch a product, train your team members, set quarterly goals, what have you. It's an incredibly short period of time, and it's getting shorter. Why? The answer is probably less than six inches from you hand right now—if you're not already reading this book on it. Smartphones and tablets have made it so much easier and quicker to share information, but the result is that

---

9   Timothy Egan, "The eight-second attention span," *The New York Times,* last modified January 22, 2016. https://www.nytimes.com/2016/01/22/opinion/the-eight-second-attention-span.html.

most of us—my audiences included—feel like they're being pulled in a million directions at once.

When I'm giving my talk on influential listening—or on just about any topic—I ask if we can take up a collection of phones, or have everyone put them away. We allow for breaks, of course, so people can check messages and make calls, but during my talk the audience has no choice but to focus.

Eight seconds. Add to that the fact that people have between thirty-five and forty-eight thoughts per minute[10] (that's about fifty thousand thoughts a day) and that most people only hear about 25 percent of what's being said,[11] and you've got a wall that's almost impossible to break down. In baseball terms, real listening is like being a .300 hitter—if you're doing it really, really well, you're basically getting about 30 percent of what's being said.

> *If you can listen—if you're able to focus and really absorb what the other person is saying, then you can learn and re-direct your thinking down paths that you never would have considered.*

If you can listen—if you're able to focus and really absorb what the other person is saying, then you can learn and re-direct your thinking down paths that you never would have considered if you'd just been waiting to ask another question instead of actually listening to the response.

---

10   Bruce Davis, "There Are 50,000 Thoughts Standing Between You and Your Partner Every Day!" blog post May 23, 2013, last modified July 23, 2013. https://www.huffingtonpost.com/bruce-davis-phd/healthy-relationships_b_3307916.html.

11   Ralph G. Nichols and Leonard A. Stevens, "Listening to People," *Harvard Business Review*, last modified September 1957, https://hbr.org/1957/09/listening-to-people.

Being an influential listener comes down to four main points:

1. Taking time to reset

2. Setting specific times to focus on one task (or person) at a time

3. Listening to understand, not reply

4. Being present and focused

TAKING TIME TO RESET

Very early on in our relationship, I freaked Paul out by talking in the shower. It wasn't so much that I was talking as that I didn't really know I was doing it. It inevitably happened right before one of my tennis games, back when I used to compete, and he'd hear me in the shower saying "Come on!" over and over again. That was my rally cry. I heard it in my head so loudly that I didn't realize that I was actually speaking the words.

"Come on!" I'd say to myself. "It's game time. Come on, you've got this!"

That pause in the shower before a game was my reset. I do the same thing now right before a presentation, just not with the shower part. It's all about taking a breath and turning your focus to one thing, be it a tennis match, speaking, or the person you're interviewing. You have to be prepared to listen and respond to what you hear, not to speak the words you're waiting to use.

Going back to the baseball analogy, why do you think there's an on-deck circle? It's for taking a few practice swings, sure, but it's also a place for batters to relax for a moment, to set their mind to what they want to do. Batters aren't jumping out of the dugout, grabbing a bat, and running up the plate. They're pausing, focusing, resetting their minds, and then putting all of their focus on the task at hand.

Running late, running into a room completely out of breath, sometimes can't be helped, but even if that happens, stop yourself, take a breath, and give yourself a moment to reset and switch your focus to the new task at hand.

> Why do you think there's an on-deck circle? It's for taking a few practice swings, sure, but it's also a place for batters to relax for a moment, to set their mind to what they want to do.

This is a practice that I live and (literally) breathe in my line of work. If I'm not present during an interview or while I'm on air, then something very serious has happened in my world. Furniture can be flying all over the house and I'll still act as if nothing is going on—it's just me, the audience, and whomever I'm speaking with. I'm able to drown out the noise— to the point where I was once able to conduct an entire show from the top of a billboard.

Of course, people have said to me, "Sure, that's easy for you to say. You listen for a living."

But don't we all? Or at least, shouldn't listening be a key part of what we do? A salesperson could miss out on a vital piece of information if they're not truly listening to a potential client. A teacher may not know how to help a pupil if they're not really listening to the student's problem. A manager may not be able to repair an issue if they're not paying full attention to what their team is saying.

Take a breath and shake off those thirty-five to forty-eight thoughts per minute. Focus on the task at hand and prepare to be completely present until that task is complete.

SET TIMES TO FOCUS ON ONE THING (OR PERSON)

I mentioned in an earlier chapter that while I enjoy lunch meetings, too many of them in a week can keep me from getting my job done. That's why, instead, I like to schedule face-to-face meetings during times like my morning walk. It's something that I would be doing anyway, only this way I can walk and meet with someone in person.

I realize that a lot of my in-person meetings could be done over the phone, and I do those a lot, sometimes having what I call "virtual coffee" with the person on the other end. But if it's possible, I prefer face-to-face because people are actually thirty-four times more effective in an in-person conversation than they are over any other communications medium.[12] This is because face-to-face allows you to connect with the other person that much more, creating a closer relationship that will benefit both of you, whether it's simply the benefit of a better connection through a good conversation or something greater, such as gaining a sale or standing out for a promotion when the opportunity arises.

Just as it's important to set aside time to focus on one person or one task, it's also critical to know when you need to reschedule that time. If you know you're going to be distracted because of another major life event or circumstances beyond your control, it's okay to reschedule. Don't make a habit of it, of course, but if you know that your focus isn't going to be 100 percent on the task at hand, consider setting another time when it will be.

LISTEN TO UNDERSTAND, NOT REPLY

As of the publication of this book, I've conducted about 16,000 interviews—possibly more. The difference between the interviews I conduct and a lot of the interviews you hear on the news or on other radio networks is that I'm all about the conversation.

I'm not waiting to ask the next question on a list. I may think of a few questions to ask before jumping into the conversation because I

---

12 Vanessa Bohns, "A Face-to-Face Request Is 34 Times More Successful Than an Email," *Harvard Business Review* website, last modified April 11, 2016, https://hbr.org/2017/04/a-face-to-face-request-is-34-times-more-successful-than-an-email.

want to be prepared, but inevitably I just follow where the conversation takes us. If I'm just waiting to ask a pre-written question, I'm almost certainly missing what the interviewee is saying, because I'm just waiting to speak.

The interviewee's answer to the question may be good, but I'm missing that sweet spot. If I'm not actually having a conversation, then I'm just being quiet until I can get my point across.

BEING PRESENT AND FOCUSED

The only way one can listen to understand is by being present and focused on the conversation. It's not the easiest mind-set to get into, but if you follow the first three points of influential listening—resetting, setting a specific time, and listening to understand—then it's much easier to pull it off.

Being present is something I've become pretty good at. If I'm not present in a conversation, then something pretty serious is happening in my world and, more than likely, I'll reschedule. I don't do it often, but when you know there's no way you're going to be able to focus on the conversation, it's best to hold it at another time. But there are few circumstances that will make me reschedule a conversation. Remember that speaking snafu I spoke about in the previous chapter that wound up with my husband and I driving seventeen hours from Dallas to Phoenix? I could have called the association up and told them I just couldn't make it, but I wasn't going to let them down. Instead, I did everything in my power to get there, and after about two hours of sleep, I walked on that stage, took a deep breath to reset, and focused on all of the interviews in front of me.

Life happens. Flights get rescheduled, clients cancel, things happen last minute, and sometimes it's all you can do to figure out what's going on in your own life, let alone take the time to focus on someone else's. But if you stop, step into the on-deck circle, and take a moment to just breathe, you'll be amazed at how much of the chaos you can let go of. The reward of discovering something new, something you never might have asked about if you were reading from a pre-written list, is more than worth the effort.

PAY ATTENTION TO THE SIGNS

Before I learned how to be an influential listener, I just let everybody run all over me all the time. As president of the National Speakers Association in Dallas, for instance, I thought I had to do everything to get ready for the year, when in fact I was wasting effort. I was letting people pull me for hours in directions that I didn't have time to go. I wasn't setting times to focus on one thing, and instead I tried to do a hundred things at once. I wasn't paying attention to the signs that I was losing quality for the sake of quantity. Boundaries are necessary—they're the key to solid, productive conversations that ultimately allow you to get far more done than you would have by scattering your efforts.

Reset. Focus. Understand. Be present. If you set these parameters, you will be much more effective in just about anything you do. It will certainly make you a better listener, and you'll connect with others better because they can tell that you're actually interested in what they have to say.

ONE LAST THOUGHT—ON REAL COMMUNICATION IN THE DIGITAL AGE

Earlier I mentioned the value of communicating face-to-face. That number—of being thirty-four times more effective in person—is likely going to go up the more we rely on digital means of communicating. When other people can see that you're present in the conversation, they're more willing to work with you. How can you convey that presence when you can't see each other?

Digitally, you can make yourself more "real" to the person you're communicating with by disrupting the normal pattern. Of course, it's still not as effective as an in-person talk or even a video conference, but the response rate is certainly better.

It all starts with the subject line. With people sending and receiving an average of 140 emails per day, a boring subject line is not going to stand out, let alone get opened. You can say something ridiculous or funny, like "My guess is the woodchuck would chuck forty-two woods, but I'm an optimist," but it's got to be unusual enough to catch the reader's eye and spark their curiosity.

The body of the email, too, should avoid the "I" pronoun like the plague. Instead, it should directly address the reader—short, sweet, and all about "you."

A good friend of mine, Meridith Elliott Powell, is great at this. She's a big-time business

> *A boring subject line is not going to stand out, let alone get opened.*

speaker who is constantly jetting around the world, so her emails are usually these quick little jots that inevitably grab my attention faster than anyone else's. In fact, I still remember the email she sent to recommend me to an organization that was looking for a speaker. She copied me on it, and the subject line read "You need to look at my friend Kate. She's awesome and she's sort of famous."

That was it. Within a day, the organization got back with me and asked if we could talk. What drove them to me was the unusual turn of the subject line, the personal connection that the phrasing created, and the line "she's sort of famous." It sparked their curiosity.

Now, I'm not a household name, but when the organization looked me up, they saw my resume and my reputation in the sports and speaking worlds and wanted to connect.

We all want to be heard, but it's rare that we feel the person we're communicating with is really listening—and the same goes with email. When you get a generic subject, generic language, you're unlikely to connect with the sender. So how do you connect? By focusing on the other person and keeping the conversation real.

I'll give you a good example. I was on my way home from a speaking engagement and was standing in the crowded Dallas-Fort Worth baggage claim waiting for my golf clubs to show up, when my phone began buzzing with emails. It was a company that wanted to connect with me about speaking, and they needed feedback ASAP, so instead of waiting until I got home to write a formal reply, I wrote them an email with the subject line "I just got off a plane so you can tell I'm writing this on my iPhone."

The body simply read, "I'm at DFW waiting for my golf clubs, which they can't seem to find. The good news is that my husband was looking for a holiday gift for me. Might be clubs.

"My wheelhouse is sales and marketing. I love it. I ran two sales departments and I've negotiated hundreds of deals. Let's schedule a call if you think I'm a good fit." That's a whole other book, but along the way and in between radio jobs, this is what I did. I know how to talk, negotiate, and I have lots of ideas. Sometimes I think we strive for perfection and we decrease our odds by waiting to get back.

It wasn't the kind of email they teach you to write in business school, but it piqued their interest, and when they wrote me back they said that they hoped my golf clubs made it back to me. It was personal, it connected, and it lead to booking a great speaking engagement.

If you can't converse in person, your emails should create a personal connection. Be real, take the time to understand the other person, and follow the rules of influential listening to create that true connection. Whether it's in person or on virtual paper, people can tell when you're really taking the time to "hear" them, or if you just consider them another distraction in a flurry of too many priorities.

PLAYMAKER: DAVID ROSS

While David Ross started his MLB career playing for the Los Angeles Dodgers, and went on to play for the Pittsburgh Pirates, San Diego Padres, Cincinnati Reds, Boston Red Sox, and Atlanta Braves, he's likely going to be remembered the most for his time with the Chicago Cubs, and more specifically for his role in Game 7 of the 2016 World Series. How do you pull off a home run after a rough start on the pitching mound? By taking a breath, resetting, and focusing.

"The half inning before, I'd let in two runs," David told me during an interview as we discussed the infamous Game 7. "I threw one in the stands and almost got [Anthony] Rizzo killed. And then the next ball hit off my mask, which let [Jason] Kipnis score all the way from second base and put runners on second and third. I'm thinking, 'What the heck? I'm supposed to be the run prevention guy. I'm not supposed to be letting these runs in.'"

These thoughts were stampeding through David's head as it came to be his turn at-bat. He was distracted, and he knew it.

"I had to regroup. I was taking the first pitch, so when I got to the batter's box, I took a breath and said, 'Okay, calm your emotions. Just take one.'

"I saw the first pitch right out of his hand—it was a heater, up and away. The next pitch he threw the same thing—middle fast ball, kind of down where I like it, and I hit it pretty good. ... It was a cool moment for me and a sense of relief after that ball went out that I got a run back after letting in two."

At thirty-nine years old, David became the oldest player to hit a home run in a World Series Game 7. It was also his last official at-bat, as he'd announced his retirement after the 2016 season several months earlier. If it hadn't been for that resetting moment that David took between letting those runs in while pitching and his final career at-bat, it's very likely that he'd never have made that home run drive down center.

Reset. Focus. Understand. Be present. Not only do these actions improve how you listen and understand those around you, they also help you keep a better perspective on life.

CURVEBALLS

How do you stay focused? Are you listening to understand instead of replying right away?

Do you ask questions when you need more information?

Are you truly connecting with people or are you keeping one eye on your phone or other devices at all times?

BE EXTRAORDINARY

Part of being extraordinary is that most people who are don't realize it.

Just look at the life of entrepreneur and self-made billionaire John Paul Jones DeJoria, cofounder of the Paul Mitchell line of hair products and Patrón Spirits. He grew up destitute, a member of a street gang with very little in the way of a future, until one day he decided that he was going to become a success and never looked back. On one of the occasions I interviewed him, John Paul told me that he credits a teacher of his for that change in perspective.

"He said that I would never succeed at anything in life," John Paul explained, and that scathing comment became the fuel for his fire. As of 2017, he was involved in too many companies to name and had a stated net worth of $3.1 billion, and in 2008 became a partner with Nelson Mandela in his Food4Africa program, which is aimed at helping to feed more than 17,000 orphaned children in Africa.

Another word that goes hand-in-hand with extraordinary is "surprising," and I believe that's because extraordinary people are unexpected—they're underestimated, plugging away at their passion until one day, when they absolutely nail whatever it is they've been pursuing—whether it's the wild success of an amazing start-up or winning the Super Bowl—it's as though the world has exploded.

Oprah Winfrey was one of those unbelievable surprises. She grew up in rural poverty, but she didn't let that slow her down. By age thirty-two, she was a millionaire and the Oprah Winfrey Show was in national syndication—and it stayed in syndication for an extraordinary twenty-five years, from 1986 to 2011. A producer, actor, philanthropist, talk show host, and all-around rainmaker, Oprah is a powerhouse and she is not done yet. As she said in her speech after receiving the Cecil B. DeMille award in 2018, there is "a new day on the horizon."

Did Oprah ever think of herself as extraordinary? Probably not. She is so busy in her world, leading her many teams, that she doesn't stop to think that she's done anything remarkable. But the world notices, and we're amazed.

There are quite a few people on my extraordinary list, and every one of them has earned my absolute admiration. They have stuck with life even when life turned its back on them, and they made something—many times, out of practically nothing.

My mom, Kathleen Delaney, is on my list—not because people are naturally obligated to acknowledge their moms, but because of how she was able to help my brother Patrick and I see what was possible and keep an open mind. What we did with our future was up to us.

Sir Richard Branson is another extraordinary individual and my personal business crush. Trendsetter, disruptor, billionaire, founder of the Virgin Group, and humanitarian, he continues to swim against the waves, shaking himself off when he fails and jumping right back in without hesitation and with all the zeal in the world.

All the people I've mentioned in this book, and many others I've met along the way, are exceptionally extraordinary people. I've learned so much from each of them, and even though I've conducted tens of thousands of interviews in my career, they have all managed to surprise me. Others, whom I wasn't able to speak to at length in the book and yet are extraordinary in their own right, include Shonda Rhimes, Billie Jean King, Meg Whitman, Elon Musk, Michael Dell, and Jerry Lurie, as well as that extraordinary organization, the National Speakers Association.

I relate to so many of these people because, like them, I was underestimated. I still am in many ways, but that's okay—it means I still get to be the surprise. I still get to be the girl who pops out of the cake.

FULL CIRCLE

At the beginning of this book, I shared my childhood story of going to see the Phillies play and cheering for the red team even though I was standing in a sea of blue. It's only appropriate, then, that this book ends with another extraordinary—and Philly-specific—event: the Eagles winning the 2018 Super Bowl.

As a kid watching the Phillies so many years ago, I could never have imagined being the host of a national sports radio show when our hometown football team made it to the Super Bowl. Everyone who listened to my show on NBC knew that I was a die-hard Eagles fan, so when they beat the Minnesota Vikings thirty-eight to seven and became the team to take on the New England Patriots, my phone never stopped ringing. I was a guest on more talk shows than I could count, and as exciting as it was, I was also a little surprised to find that not a single one of those show hosts thought that the Eagles had a fighting chance.

"If the Eagles don't win, hey, it's just great how far they got, right?" was a common sentiment. But I refused to agree with them.

Sure, they were the underdogs, and yes, their star quarterback was injured, but they were scrappy, and I knew they were going to win.

Super Bowl LII was one of the most extraordinary games I've ever had the privilege to watch, not in small part due to the incredible showing by quarterback Nick Foles, who was filling in for injured MVP candidate Carson Wentz. With three touchdowns, 373 passing yards, and actually receiving an additional touchdown, Foles became the first quarterback in sixteen years to start the season as a backup and go on to win a championship.

"People don't know who Nick Foles is," said Nick's dad, Larry Foles, in a *Sports Illustrated* interview following the game. "He's the kind of guy that can sneak up on you."[13]

That's being extraordinary. For Nick, he was just doing what he loved and working hard at that passion every day. And that's the dirty little secret to becoming extraordinary: it doesn't just come out of left field. It takes a massive amount of grit, guts, and determination. You know you're headed in the right direction when you're losing sleep, friends, and track of time because you're so absorbed in pursuing what you love. And that feeling when you accomplish your goal—the thrill, the bone-deep exhaustion, the deep sense of reward after countless hours of invested time and tears—is indescribable. If I could bottle that emotion up and sell it, I'd be richer than Amazon's Jeff Bezos! But it has to be earned, and in earning it, the world is very likely to suddenly discover the extraordinary you.

If you truly want to deal your own destiny and become extraordinary, then you have to go all in. You have to dig deeper to connect

---

13   "A Play Call for the Ages and a (Backup) QB That Amazes: How the Eagles Won Super Bowl LII," *Sports Illustrated,* last modified February 12, 2017, https://www. si.com/nfl/2018/02/06/super-bowl-2018-eagles-patriots-nick-foles-doug-pederson-howie-roseman greg-bishop-and-ben-baskin.

more powerfully with current and future clients, and you have to do it continuously. Patience pays. I challenge you to adopt crucial long-game thinking and realistic goal setting. And along the way, there's nothing wrong with stacking the deck—really surrounding yourself with advocates, mentors, and successful leaders in other industries—because these are the people who are going to remind you that there's a light at the end of the tunnel—and that there might be faster and better ways of getting there.

Even though there were many times in my life when I thought the glass ceiling was too hard and that it was never going to crack, I can look back now and say that it was all worth it. I could have taken an easier road, and believe me, I've been tempted to, but I know that deep down, I never would have felt as satisfied. All the amazing people I've met and all the places I've been allowed to go where others couldn't have been worth it.

> *That feeling when you accomplish your goal—the thrill, the bone-deep exhaustion, the deep sense of reward after countless hours of invested time and tears—is indescribable.*

Ignore the critics. Go high when others go low. Surround yourself with advocates, and above all, don't let anyone but you deal your destiny.

SPEAKING AND CONSULTING SERVICES

Want to be heard? Kate Delaney has three million listeners that tune in to hear her every week. She has interviewed Fortune 500 CEOs and discovered their untold secrets to becoming successful. Make sure your next conference, meeting, or event includes Kate Delaney's insights on achieving bold, high-level, and dramatic results in your professional life.

MEDIA CONSULTING

Delaney Media Group (DMG) helps corporations and individuals expand their visibility and influence for bigger profits. We've partnered with countless entrepreneurs and corporations to make their message stand out. DMG delivers custom media and marketing coaching and workshops for dozens of law firms, speakers, sales teams, companies, and sports teams. We also specialize in event media and marketing to create more opportunities for you to get in front of your target clients. Kate and crew will travel to you or plan to join us in Dallas.

To check Kate's availability or to learn more about her speaking engagements, contact Paul Joslin at Paul@katedelaneyspeaker.com or call Delaney Media Group at (469) 777-1054.

CONNECT WITH KATE!

Facebook: katedelaneyfanpage

Twitter: @katesdelaney

LinkedIn: Kate Delaney

Email: k8@katedelaneyspeaker.com,
kate@dealyourowndestiny.com

Website: www.dealyourowndestiny.com